RELIGION AND ETHNICITY

Essays by

Harold Barclay
Harold Coward
Frank Epp
David Goa
Yvonne Yazbeck Haddad

Gordon Hirabayashi
Roger Hutchinson
Leslie Kawamura
Grant Maxwell
Cyril Williams

Edited by

Harold Coward and Leslie Kawamura

Published for
The Calgary Institute for the Humanities
by
Wilfrid Laurier University Press

Canadian Cataloguing in Publication Data

Workshop on Religion and Ethnicity, University
of Calgary, 1977.
Religion and ethnicity

Workshop held August 8-12, 1977.

ISBN 0-88920-064-5 pa.

1. Canada - Religion - Congresses. 2. Minorities
- Canada - Congresses. I. Barclay, Harold.
II. Coward, Harold G., 1936- III. Kawamura,
Leslie, 1935- IV. Calgary Institute for the
Humanities. V. Title.

BL2530.C2W67 1977 200'.971 C78-001081-7

Wilfrid Laurier University Press
Waterloo, Ontario, Canada
N2L 3C5

TABLE OF CONTENTS

INTRODUCTORY NOTE

The papers in this volume were originally presented at a Workshop on Religion and Ethnicity held at the University of Calgary from August 8 - 12, 1977. This Workshop was sponsored by the Calgary Institute for the Humanities. The Institute was founded in 1976 to foster the growth of humanistic research at the University of Calgary. This volume is one of a series which the Institute hopes to publish in the fulfillment of this objective.

It gives us great pleasure to acknowledge the financial assistance of The Canada Council which helped to defray the costs of the Workshop. In addition grateful acknowledgement is due to Harold Coward and Leslie Kawamura for their organizational and editorial labours, and to Mrs. Geraldine Dyer for the preparation of the manuscript. All the contributors also deserve our warmest thanks for helping to make the Workshop a very congenial and academically valuable occasion, the quality of which is well reflected in the essays which follow.

We are especially grateful to Alberta Culture and its Minister, the Honourable Horst Schmid, for a grant in support of publication of this volume.

Terence Penelhum,
Director

ABOUT THE AUTHORS

Harold B. Barclay is the acting chairman, Department of Anthropology, University of Alberta, Edmonton. He holds a Ph.D. in Anthropology from Cornell University (1961) and has taught at the American University (Cairo, Egypt), Knox College (Galesburg, Illinois), the University of Oregon, and the University of Alberta. He has been a visiting professor at the University of Texas and the University of California (Berkeley). Among his publications are *Buurri Al Lomaab: A Suburban Village in the Sudan* (Cornell Press, 1964), and many articles including "An Arab Muslim Community in the Canadian Northwest: The Lebanese Community in Lac La Biche, Alberta," in *Minority Canadians*, J. L. Elliott, ed., (Prentice Hall, 1971).

Harold G. Coward is Associate Dean of the Faculty of Humanities, University of Calgary. He holds a Ph.D. in Indian philosophy and religion from McMaster University (1973). He has been a visiting Research Scholar at the Center for the Advanced Study of Philosophy, Benares Hindu University, where he studied under T. R. V. Murti. He is the author of *Sphoṭa Theory* (Motilal Banarsidaas, 1976) and *Bhartṛhari* (Twayne, 1976) and of many articles including his forthcoming "Psychological Epistemology" in *Genetic Psychology Monographs* (early in 1978).

Frank Epp is President and Associate Professor of History, Conrad Grebel College, University of Waterloo. He holds a Ph.D. in History from the University of Minnesota (1965) and an Honorary LL.D. from Brandon University (1975). He is the founding editor of the *Canadian Mennonite* and the *Mennonite Reporter* and has held part-time pastorates in Winnipeg, Minneapolis, Altona, and Ottawa. He is the author of *Mennonite Exodus: The Rescue and Resettlement of the Russian Mennonites Since the Communication Revolution* (D. W. Friesen & Sons, 1962), *The Palestinians: Portrait of a People in Conflict* (McClelland and Stewart, 1976), and of many other books and articles. He has travelled widely visiting Vietnam, other Asian countries and Russia (1966), Western Europe (1977), the Middle East (1960-74), Latin America (1972) and USSR and Indonesia (1976).

David J. Goa is Curator of Folk Life (Ethnic and Cultural Studies), Provincial Museum of Alberta, Edmonton. He has supervised the research and writing of *Preliminary Report on the Material Folk Culture of the German-Speaking Population of Alberta* (by Eckehart and Monica Maremholtz) and other historical and cultural surveys including *Alberta's Icelandic Community, Alberta's Danish Community,* and *Alberta's Japanese Community* (by Margret Calder). He has organized many exhibits among which are *The Spiritual Life of Albertans* (a permanent gallery at the Provincial Museum) and *All Things Common* (a feature exhibit on the religious meaning of Hutterite Material Culture), and a major travelling exhibit circulated by the Devonian Foundation (1974-78) titled, *Peoples of Alberta.* He has given numerous talks related to the issues of immigration and to the cultural and religious life of Alberta's ethnic communities.

Yvonne Yazbeck Haddad is a Research Assistant at the Institute of Islamic Studies at McGill University. She is presently in the process of completing her Ph.D. in the History of Religions (Islamic) under the guidance of Dr. Issa Boullata. She has lectured widely at the University of Calgary, North-eastern University (Boston), Vassar College (Poughkeepsic, N. Y.), Hartford Seminary Foundation (Connecticut), Aleppo College (Syria), and the American School for Girls (Beirut, Lebanon). Among her many publications are "The Conception of the Term *Dīn* in the Qur'ān," *The Muslim World* (LXIV, No. 2, 1974) and "Women in the Afterlife: The Islamic View as Seen from Qur'ān and Traditions," (co-authored with Jane Smith), *Journal of the American Academy of Religion* (XLIII, No. 1, 1975).

Gordon Hirabayashi is a Professor of Sociology, University of Alberta, Edmonton. He holds a Ph.D. in Sociology from the University of Washington, Seattle (1952) and has taught at the University of Washington, the American University of Beirut (Lebanon), and the American University of Cairo (Egypt). He has served various roles in various organizations as consultant (Canadian Citizenship Branch, Edmonton), as a Board of Director (Canadian Native Friendship Centre, Edmonton), as Consulting Editor (Social Science and Medicine), and as Chairman (Japanese Canadian Centennial Society). Among his publications are *Industrialization in Alexandria: Some Social and Ecological Aspects* (with Hassan el-Saaty, Cairo, American University Press, 1959) and many articles including "Doukhobor Social Organization," *The Doukhobors of British Columbia,* Hawthorn ed., (U.B.C., 1952) and "The Japanese Interment Camp: Can it Happen Again?" *Bridge* (Vol. 4, No. 5, November, 1976).

Roger Hutchinson is an Assistant Professor, Department of Religious Studies, Victoria College, University of Toronto, Ontario. He holds a Th.D. in Christian Ethics from the Toronto School of Theology at the University of Toronto (1975). He has been a consultant for the Inter-church Project on Population, and has presented papers on social ethics and the population policy debate for the Ecumenical Forum, Toronto; the Institute for Environmental Studies, U. of T.; the Centre for Christian Studies, Toronto; and the American Society of Christian Ethics. His publications include: "The Canadian Social Gospel in the Context of Christian Social Ethics," "Inflation Has Moral Implications," and "Religion, Morality and Law in Modern Canada."

Leslie S. Kawamura is an Assistant Professor, Department of Religious Studies, University of Calgary, Alberta. He holds a Ph.D. from the University of Saskatchewan, Saskatoon, in Far Eastern Studies (1974). He has studied at the Kyoto University (Japan) and has taught at the Nyingma Institute (Berkeley), Institute of Buddhist Studies (Berkeley), and the University of Saskatchewan (Saskatoon). Among his publications are *Mind in Buddhist Psychology* (with H. V. Guenther, Dharma Press, 1975), *Golden Zephyr* (Dharma Press, 1975) and articles including "Nairātmya--No Self?" *Shambhala Review* (Vol. 5, Nos. 1-2) and "Buddhist Churches in Alberta" (forthcoming) *Religions in Canada,* Peter Slater, ed. He was a founding member of the Honpa Buddhist Church of Alberta and the Canada-Mongolia Society.

J. Grant Maxwell is a native of the Prairies and was raised on a farm near Plenty, Saskatchewan. He graduated from St. Thomas More College, University of Saskatchewan. During the latter years of the 2nd World War, he served as a member of the Naval reserve service. He has worked as a reporter and commentator with the radio, press and television in the 1950s and early 1960s. He was active in the Christian Family Movement, 1956-1966, both locally and internationally. He has served as Lay Director, Catholic Centre, Saskatoon (1960-68); as English-language director of Social Affairs, Canadian Conference of Catholic Bishops (1969-76); as a Consultor with the Pontifical Commission Justice & Peace, Vatican City (1972-75); and as designer of an experiment in social journalism PROJECT FEEDBACK (1974-76).

Cyril G. Williams is Reader in Religious Studies and Head of Religious Studies, University College of Wales (Aberystweyth). He has served as a Professor of Religion and as the Chairman of the Department of Religion at Carleton University, as an External Examiner in Religious Studies for the University of Stirling; and as a Chief Examiner in Religious Knowledge for the Welsh Joint-Education Committee. Among his published works are *Clywsoch Yr Enw* (Modern Religious Thought, Modern Welsh Publication, 1966), *Nadolig yn Calcutta* (Fomer, 1975) and numerous articles. He has visited Palestine on an archaeological study and also India.

PREFACE

The religious life of mankind is full of paradoxes. Not the least of these is the fact that although our faiths make universal claims, each faith is intensely culture-bound in its forms. The questions to which this gives rise are as urgent as they are fascinating. We may feel compelled to ask how far the variety of religious forms casts doubt on the validity of the claims made within them; or how far the variety is merely a mask for a deeper unity in the claims themselves. But in addition to these questions of philosophy and theology, we can be driven, either as students of society or as members of a faith, to investigate the ways in which the forms of religious life we know are related to the times and communities in which they are found. It is to this investigation that the studies in this volume are contributions.

With one exception they all deal with the relationship between living religious traditions in Canada and the fabric of Canadian society. Canada is a pluralistic society, ethnically and religiously. How are these two pluralisms related? Their connection is intimate, but never simple. For many years there could plausibly have been said to be a dominant Anglo-Canadian Protestant tradition, with other faiths and denominations being associated primarily with ethnic minorities. No doubt this would always have been a simplistic understanding; but today, as Canadian culture is increasingly secularised, it is religion itself, not just some special forms of it, that the majority tends to see as a minority concern. Ethnic and religious loyalties pull together against a secular assimilation--an unequal contest which is also matched elsewhere, as Cyril Williams reminds us in his essay. Such a change leaves the "establishment" denominations with an unwanted identity-crisis of their own, not the least part of which is due to an unfamiliar awareness of their own ethnic roots and histories.

The essays were originally presented at a week-long summer workshop at the University of Calgary. Those present at the discussions they generated were conscious of participating in an enquiry which urgently needs to be broadened and deepened. It is a commonplace that Canadians have been forced by circumstances into reflecting more than any other

nation on the sort of diversity that is compatible with their nationhood. It is high time we came to understand the ways religion has
contributed to the problem, and can contribute to its solution.

Harold Coward
Leslie Kawamura

SECULARIZATION AMONG ETHNIC COMMUNITIES IN WESTERN CANADA

> Hear the word of the Lord, O house of Jacob, and all
> the families of the house of Israel. Thus says the
> Lord: 'What wrong did your fathers find in me that
> they went far from me, and went after worthlessness
> and became worthless?' They did not say, 'Where is
> the Lord who brought us up from the land Egypt, who
> led us in the wilderness, in a land of deserts and
> pits, in a land of drought and deep darkness, in a
> land that none passes through, where no man dwells?'
>
> And I brought you into a plentiful land, to enjoy
> its fruits and its good things. But when you came
> in you defiled my land, and made my heritage an
> abomination. The priests did not say, 'Where is
> the Lord?' Those who handle the law did not know
> me; the rulers transgressed against me; the pro-
> phets prophesied by Ba'al and went after things
> that do not profit.
>
> Has a nation changed its gods, even though they are
> no gods? But my people have changed their glory
> for that which does not profit.

At this point my friend the Rabbi raised his voice, finishing the
quotation with a passion matching that of the prophet.

> Be appalled, O heavens, at this, be shocked, be
> utterly desolate, says the Lord, for my people
> have committed two evils: they have forsaken
> me, the fountain of living waters, and hewed
> out cisterns for themselves, broken cisterns
> that can hold no water.
>
> *Jeremiah* 2:4-8, 11-13. RSV

We had been talking rather casually about the community he served
as teacher for some forty years. I had begun to probe the vitality of
the community when his gentle spirit exploded into the Hebrew of Jere-
miah. Only when he had completed the passage did he enquire if I
understood the language. His freewheeling translation followed, and
then a rabbinical gloss pointing out that the first evil, "they have
forgotten me" paled in sight of the second, "and hewed out cisterns
for themselves". With a face that suggested this whole issue had
caused him some pain, he went on to recount how, throughout his years
of service, up through the early 1950s, the men in the community would
gather to read *Torah* and ponder their life together with a directness
that in recent years simply did not exist. Now the community's primary concerns were the details of rite; the jot and tittle of the law.

Previously, this was merely accepted as a skeletal structure which gave opportunity to ponder the way of Torah. Now the way was primarily to do what was required, complete it and have done. This attitude he identified with the "broken cisterns" that give one the sensation of being refreshed when in fact one is being poisoned.

Expressions such as this are a commonplace pointing to the experience covered by the umbrella term, secularization, that has come about since the 15th century. I would like to draw our attention to the larger historical and cultural factors involved in this concern, to briefly highlight the particular circumstances of immigrant life in Western Canada that exacerbates this situation, and, finally, to illustrate with several examples the particular complexities that shroud the lives of so many, and perhaps of us all.

Secularity has received considerable attention over the last decade. Most of the sociological literature has been concerned with its growth, extent, and direction, and has let stand the presupposition that secularity is indeed commonplace. The problem is simply that little attention has been given to what is meant by secularization.

The framework within which the discussion of secularity has taken place has been nicely summarized by Joan Brothers around three assumptions.[1] It has been generally assumed: first, that the territory of the sacred and that of the profane can be easily marked out and that we would then be looking at two quite distinct topographies; secondly, that primitive cultures can be idealized as religious while industrial cultures are incurably secular; and, finally, that religious experience is identifiable with participation in institutionalized religion.

In all three assumptions, the discussion is fixed by idealizations quite apart from the normative experience of any community. There are few individuals or communities who would accept the first assumption, the separation of their sacred world from their profane one. The great proliferation of religious expressions among the young in North America flies in the face of the second assumption, that industrial culture is thoroughly secular. Identifying religious experience with participation in institutional forms of a faith, the third assumption, is perhaps useful when those forms are the center and boundary of a people, for example, an ethnic community. But it becomes ridiculous as a model for discussion in a large part of the industrialized world where "community" has undergone a drastic metamorphosis.

The obvious difficulty in this discussion is that secularity and religion are set off against each other in a way that is quite irrelevant to the life of people. It tells us more about the intellectuals preoccupation with their own secular purity than it does about the communities under discussion.

Clifford Geertz has suggested that:

> We look not for a universal property--'sacredness' or 'belief in the supernatural', for example-- that divides religious phenomena off from non-religious ones with Cartesian sharpness, but for a system of concepts that can sum up a set of inexact similarities, which are yet genuine similarities, we sense to inhere in a given body of material. We are attempting to articulate a way of looking at the world, not to describe an unusual object.[2]

I would suggest that a similar point of view govern the search to locate secularity, that we look not for a "universal property" and that the attempt be to "articulate a way of looking at the world", or, perhaps, "ways of avoiding a world".

All mankind must pass through the gates of childhood and upon initiation into adult life discover the new dimensions of meaning that encompass innocence and its loss. This normal process has for most of mankind taken place within one dynamic mythic world that makes sense out of experience. In the modern world this process takes place on the margins between numerous mythical and idealogical systems, all vying to mediate experience. This leads to a preoccupation with the meaning of these various interpretive systems. Traditional man, given his dynamic mythology, is led directly into the ambiguities of his experience. We tend to get hung up interminably in the ambiguities of the possible ways of understanding the experience.

Secularity, as I will use it, suggests the grey areas that develop in the minds and hearts of men when they find themselves being nurtured by mythologies that are at a cultural interface.

The historical movement that led to this fundamental sense of homelessness[3] has been elaborated on by numerous capable scholars. Briefly, I would like, with the help of Hannah Arendt, to sketch a central historical factor, a keystone in the human condition of modern man. She suggests in a most persuasive manner:

> ...that property, as distinguished from wealth and appropriation, indicates the privately owned share of a common world and therefore is the most elementary political condition for man's worldliness. By

> the same token, expropriation and world aliena-
> tion coincide, and the modern age, very much
> against the intentions of all the actors in the
> play, began by alienating certain strata of the
> population from the world. We tend to overlook
> the central importance of this alienation for the
> modern age, because we usually suggest its secular
> character and identify the term secularity with
> worldliness. Yet secularization as a tangible
> historical event means no more than separation
> of church and state, of religion and politics....
> A return to the early Christian attitude of 'ren-
> der to Caesar the things that are Caesar's and
> unto God the things that are God's' rather than
> loss of faith and transcendence or a new and em-
> phatic interest in the things of this world.
>
> Modern loss of faith is not religious in origin--
> cannot be traced to the Reformation and Counter
> Reformation...and its scope is by no means re-
> stricted to the religious sphere.... The evidence
> shows that modern men were not thrown back upon
> this world but upon themselves.

She picks up Weber's thesis and reminds us that this precisely is
the origin of capitalism:

> ...that an enormous, strictly mundane activity is
> possible without any care for, or enjoyment of,
> the world whatever, an activity whose deepest mo-
> tivation, on the contrary, is worry and care about
> the self. World alienation, and not self-alienation
> as Marx thought, has been the hallmark of the modern
> age.[4]

With this sensibility the modern age came into being. The discipline of science burst forth with its tremendous concern for perpetuating a technology that affects the world, albeit, a world we are
distant from. New economic and political systems followed. Democracy,
freed man from concrete political involvements. A capitalist economic
system redefined social worth in strictly private terms and established money as the new symbol of social reality. All these factors, as
many have argued, were dependent on a dispassionate distance from the
world.[5]

While this tremendous change is happening in Europe, the New
World is "discovered" in the imagination of Europeans. This is the
backdrop against which the settlement of the New World takes place.
Its direct effect and implications are woven through the lives of all
those who settled here. Some came from the heartland of this new
modern "culture", others came to escape a life of forced agricultural
and industrial labor. They all came in search of land.

Immigration to Western Canada was encouraged by a constant flow
of publications originating in the office of the Minister of the Interior, the Honorable Clifford Sifton. The majority of these booklets
consists of brief introductions to Western Canada giving particulars
on agricultural conditions, customs, and immigration, and on the railway. The bulk of each publication is reprinted testimonials of settlers telling of the opportunity available in Western Canada. The cover was often adorned with a harvest goddess figure, a few stems of well
headed-out wheat in her left hand and a horn of plenty in her right
(Fig. 1). Golden coins flow smoothly out of the horn of plenty drift-
ing down on the prairie landscape as she dances her way across the
sky.[6] The mythology and values that permeate these publications cul-
minate in a book of cartoons Sifton published in December 1903.[7] It
opens with John Bull and Uncle Sam hastily marching to Canada with
their investments of pounds and dollars. The caricatured portrait of
Western Canada's rich possibilities is interrupted with "The Only Draw-
back", a cartoon depicting Uncle Sam remarking to Mr. Bull, "They say
it's a fine looking country, John, but durn it all, you can't see it
for the wheat" (Fig. 2). The story culminates with Jack Canuck, choir
master, leading all ethnic settlers, who stand knee-deep in wheat, in
"The Maple Leaf Forever" (Fig. 3). Several cartoons follow showing
Canada as the bread-basket and sustainer of Mother England, and as the
superior in economic rivalry with the United States.

The conclusion interests me--two cartoons depict the "myth" that
was to attract so many Europeans and Orientals to Canada. The first
shows a rugged Scot, having just come off the boat, planting a seed-
ling, a dollar sign, in the fertile Canadian soil (Fig. 4). It is
dated 1890. The companion picture shows the full grown fruit tree.
Again, it has the structure of a dollar sign, bearing cattle, horses,
children, wheat, and a large mansion-like home. A stately gentleman
stands gazing at it. He's a country gentleman who dismounted a finely
bred steed to gaze upon his tree of life.

The back cover has a similar diptych with the new prairie home in
1893 (Fig. 5). It's a cottage. The two-horse plow cuts a pleasing
furrow, while in the foreground the lady in pristine cleanliness,
sporting a floral bonnet, picks berries for dessert; they certainly
aren't for preserves. Depicted below, in 1903, ten years later, the
couple sit in their democrat and proudly survey their "labour". A
two-storey mansion stands where the cottage once was. A huge barn and

stable, with a fine herd of cattle, grace the background. The harvesting is well underway, being nicely handled this year by the seven bind-
ers, manned no doubt, by the hired men.

This is the image: land, money, independence, and the right to
leisure and status that comes from ten years of wholesome work.

The immigration to and settlement of North America is one of the
most remarkable occurrences in human history. Its mark was deeply
felt by those who took the journey, and by those who stayed behind.
The social and economic development of the New World gave the historical trends established in Europe new impetus.

There is a series of very specific characteristics that mark the
structure organized religious life had to take in North America. H.
Richard Niebhur, in his classic study of *The Social Sources of Denominationalism* (New York, 1975) has outlined them. What follows, largely stands in his debt.

Immigration attracts individuals whose ambition and need are
strong enough to demand their break with settled patterns and the com-
fortableness at home. They are mostly young and often moving out from
parental structures. I think it is fair to say they have a high degree
of independence, if not at the outset of their journey, certainly as a
consequence of it. On the prairies this married well with the individualism of the frontier.

Democracy and free land are perhaps the primary characteristics
that appealed to immigrants and that made their journey possible.
"These offered a situation in which immigrant groups were able to develop freely and to assert their specific character. But they also
provided the circumstances which made Americanization possible through
the free incorporation of the new groups in the social whole."[8] The
thorough-going separation of church and state unique to Canada and the
United States allowed for each expression of faith to flourish at will.
This also places all immigrant churches in an environment where there
was constant competition for the allegiance of parishioners and the
continual demand for justifying this allegiance. While this is a traditional part of Protestant Evangelical faiths, now given the shift in
the established norm, it becomes the necessity of all religious per-
suasions. Now, at least officially, no one was born into a religious
body. All affiliations were intentional.

This process Niebuhr calls "religious Americanization" and it has
been the lot, not only of Christian faiths, but of the Oriental

religions as well. Barkley for example has noted the Islamic community at Lac La Biche's desire and insistence that their Imam adopt a
lifestyle similar to that of the neighbouring Christian ministers.[9]
His function as Imam must now conform to the established model. In
the worship service of the Jodo Shinshu community at Raymond a conscious concern to "relate" their forms to those found in the neighbouring Christian churches is evident. The use of "hymns" and "choruses"
freely rendered into a Buddhist language frame is a simple example.

    Among immigrant churches in general there is a tendency to adopt
attitudes and practices of those already established in the community.

    The pioneer life also required an activistic approach to the
world if one was going to "make it". The Puritan backdrop to much of
North American religious style emphasized work and a very activistic
concept of God. Niebuhr suggests that many religious traditions which
"regard the essence of Christianity as doctrine and the field of Christian life as contemplation and devotion have often assumed, under the
influence of environment and tradition, that pragmatic attitude toward
their faith which characterizes American christianity".[10] In much of
Protestantism this has led to a revivalistic stance with the result
being that the bulk of the church's energy is poured into winning
souls for the church.[11] The obvious result is that little serious effort has been directed towards nurturing the community in the broad
mythology of the faith and a process of ideological selection has
taken place. This selection has occurred on the grounds outlined
above and traditions have shrunk drastically.

    A further effect of voluntary church membership has been a "theo-
logical movement in immigrant churches which turns from dogmatism towards mysticism and rationalism. It has been necessary for them to
stress personal immediacy in religion to emphasize the individual appropriation of the gospel in feeling or intellect rather than to rely
on social authority."[12] Positivistic interpretations of religion became the norm since it's easier to argue for the utility of a faith
than for its metaphysical truth.

    The democratic stance of Canada and the United States along with
the separation of church and state required a change in the customary
stance of religions toward secular governments. The politically aligned churches of Europe have become non-political while the sectarian
movements who argued a separation of ecclesiastical and secular power
have tended to speak for the state as the "power ordained by God".

Language, so closely tied to the heart of religion, has been a vivid battle ground reflecting the issues of ethnicity and secularization. Within the Franco-Albertan community until perhaps ten years ago, the phrase, *"Qui perd sa langue, perd sa foi"* (He who loses his language, loses his faith) was often heard in both parlor and pulpit. The language which spoke about the mundane world was seen as a vector to the divine. To lose it was to most certainly step outside of the mother community and to do that was to step outside the generally accepted realm of faith.

The history, the innuendo and connotation, the poetic power of a word or phrase is rightly valued by a people. The ocean of meaning present in a mother tongue finds its most sensitive expression in devotional vocabulary. It has often been the case that the leadership within an ethnic church, seeing the high possibility of extinction will opt for the working language of the society. Ethnicity is tossed aside and the religion salvaged on a narrow base of beliefs and liturgical style. With this the devotional power of the word is lost to several generations of the faithful. While church leadership is concerned to have a language that can attract membership in a competitive religious marketplace, the community with its roots in the devotional power of the word is concerned with a language that enshrines meaning and illuminates the unspeakable.

The language issue takes a particular turn in many ethnic communities bound by strong Protestant religious tradition. A broad section of the Mennonite community can serve to illustrate my point.

The Mennonite Conference and Mennonite Brethren came to North America from Russia having experienced the loss of their prosperous farming communities. A number of their leaders were also taken during the Revolution of 1917. To many of the immigrants from this period with whom I have spoken, the reason for their "chastisement by God at the hands of the Communists" has its roots in their initial settlement in Russia. The arrangement that brought the Mennonites to Russia required that they refrain from proselytizing the local peasantry. The state church wanted no competition. The Mennonites were forced by the severe European persecutions to agree to this arrangement although it countered their understanding of the New Testament injunction to evangelize all the world including one's neighbour. The communities in Russia opted for supporting foreign missions heavily and resigned themselves to a silent witness by their actions in the face of their Russian neighbours. In North America the weight of their loss, along with their sense of guilt over ignoring the call to evangelize, became strong. But here they were also isolated by language and could not proclaim the gospel unless perchance, their neighbours spoke German.

I would like to suggest that the American style of non-denominational fundamentalism that flourished through the first half of this century was a key factor in what has resulted.

Numerous Bible schools have operated throughout Western Canada, the most notable being Prairie Bible Institute at Three Hills, Alberta. Mr. L. E. Maxwell founded the school in 1921-1922 at the request of a local farmer who wanted a "Bible-centered-education" for his children. Maxwell, along with a troupe from P.B.I., regularly toured the ethnic churches that had an evangelical bent. They came with a "simple gospel message", the hymnology of frontier America and a Biblical literalism that was hard to question particularly across language barriers.

My thesis is simply that the Mennonite desire to find an evangelical stance, a stance according to many long overdue, and the non-denominational fundamentalist movement's command of English, married. The result was some satisfaction in Mennonite communities that the long lost evangelism was recovered and that finally they were responding to the world's cry for the salvation story. For the fundamentalists it provided a constituency from which students could be recruited for the Bible schools.

With the second great War, a substantial number of eligible Mennonite young men entered the armed services. Since Mennonite history is largely that of a people chased through half of Europe for their pacifism, this was a serious shift in behaviour. It contradicted a central tenet of the faith and an explanation was sought.

The community was forced to take seriously its loss of influence in the spiritual training of its children. This had fallen into the hands of non-denominational schools which didn't share Mennonite doctrine and certainly not their reading of Scripture regarding ethical behaviour. On the issue of the war they were diametrically opposed.

To sum up, the Mennonites were pulled at least in part into the American fundamentalist camp because of a need to identify with an evangelizing agent. American fundamentalism taught them an English religious language and reshaped their religious sensibilities with its music and style. The historical referents shifted as did their "hierography". Moody became a household name vying with that of Menno

Simon. Along with a long series of doctrinal controversies and disputes over ethical behaviour, the Mennonites found differing mythologi-
cal systems in their midst. They had arrived in the New World.

Perhaps the most dramatic shift in mythologies has been precipitated by technological developments. These changes have had a marked
influence on both ethnicity and religion in Western Canada. Although
an exploration of this issue is beyond our immediate concern several
examples will highlight the profound impact it can have on a community.

The route of the railroads during their development lead to the
creation and destruction of many communities virtually overnight. It
linked them to agricultural markets and to the sources of consumer
goods.

In the 1920s the construction of a spur line north from Innisfail
to Rocky Mountain House was projected. The Danish community at Dickson, fifteen miles north of Innisfail anticipated this decision and
encouraged a group of recent arrivals from Denmark to settle in the
Caroline district twenty miles further north. The rail line was never
built. As a result this small group of settlers isolated by culture
from their immediate neighbors, Americans, lived as an enclave away
from the 'mother' community at Dickson. To a man they remained, lived
out a very simple and frugal life, never married and from sources interviewed in Dickson,[13] never achieved full participation in the Danish
community.

A further example with a slightly different twist comes from the
Hutterite Brethren Community. The Hutterites have a 'cannon' of sermons, the earliest dating from 1585,[14] which are read in Hoch Deutch
according to a Sunday and Holiday pericope. Of this fixed group of
exhortations (*Aufmunterung*) perhaps two hundred were bequeathed by
Andreas Ehrenpreis, c. 1650, and the group that gathered around him.
A few sermons were added as late as 1677. A South Dakota Hutterite
preacher when asked why there were no sermons added in recent years,
criptically answered, "Can you write a love story if you have not yourself experienced true love? How can you write a true sermon if you
have never experienced suffering?"[15] Thus it has been the practise to
copy and recopy but not to add sermons to this 'cannonical' body.

The sermon is delivered verbatim by the colony preacher. He is
chosen from the brethren by a system of nomination and casting of lot.
Upon election he must begin the work of copying the "cannonical" sermons into booklets for his own use. A brother preacher's copy is

borrowed and the newly elected *Diener des Wortes* (servant of the Word)
spends the long winter evenings copying out the texts.

This necessary task occupied the winter evenings for a number of
years. It gave the scribe additional exposure to the text with its
rich use of scripture, historical reference to Anabaptist history and
"sharp" exhortation to the disciplined path of the gospels. Additional
"souls" were involved proof reading the newly copied text. The complete text was checked twice against the original manuscript with all
scripture references given a third reading in comparison with Luther's
translation of the Bible.

On a northern Alberta colony this scribe's task was in part taken
over by a sister to the newly chosen preacher.[16] She made friendly
complaints about having to provide the ink for scribing even though
her brother-preacher supplied the paper. She explicitly told me that
these texts under no circumstance could be mechanically reproduced
(typed or printed) hand copying was the only acceptable form of repro-
duction. The Brethren are skilled in the printing trade and possess
all the necessary equipment, consequently this choice is deliberate.

Later in conversation, however, it was revealed that on another
colony one of the brethren had recently acquired a photocopy machine.[17]
They suggested that since this produced the text in its original "written" form the folk mores governing the scribing of sermon's was not
contravened.

This process however removes the ritual of scribing the sermons
from the winter's activities. The immediate and direct consequence
is that several people will simply not be as exposed to the sermon
tradition and the scripture as was required by the "ritual of scribing".

Although there is no comment in the literature available to me
about how the Brethren formulated this practice I would suggest that as
with many traditional societies, the vectors used for forming individuals in the tradition and faith were often justified by recourse to
necessity. At some point in Hutterite history it was necessary to copy
sermon texts and pass them on from hand to hand.

When the physical necessity to do this is removed by the presence
of photocopying equipment the primary function of the copying, that is,
nurturing those whose task it was to copy, is forgotten.

The Hutterite experience is comparable to the loss of the tradition of storytelling within so many cultures. This is painfully

illustrated by reading the Mercury Series Reports from the Canadian
Center for Folk Culture Studies of the National Museum of Man.[18] In
all the surveys carried out so far in Western Canadian ethnic communities, the tradition of folk and children's stories, a central method
of nurturing young and old in the myth, has almost completely dried
up. The demands of modern life with its reliance on sophisticated
communications technology, a public education system and forms of
entertainment shaped by the secular humanism of the dominant culture
militate against the maintenance of traditional methods of religious
formation.

In conclusion, I would like to point out that a broad look at
ethnic/religious communities in Western Canada reveals great ambiguity
about the place and meaning of tradition. This ambiguity has reached
the foundations of all ethnic and religious communities. Perhaps a
hard look at the ethnic/religious matrix, sketching in detail the way
myth, ideology and history have converged, would give a cleaner sense
of what it is that perplexes.

Figure 1

Figure 2

Figure 3

Figure 4

Figure 5

FOOTNOTES

1. *The Persistence of Religion*, ed. Andrew Greeley and Gregory Baum
   (New York: Herder and Herder, 1973), pp. 46-57. The following
   are germane to the thrust of this paper: "Religion in a Secular
   Society," Andrew Greeley, *Social Research*, Vol. 41 (1974), pp.
   226-240. "Religion in Postindustrial America: The Problem of
   Secularization," Talcott Parsons, *Social Research*, Vol. 41 (1974),
   pp. 193-225. "Secularism as the Common Religion of a Free Soci-
   ety," Horace M. Kallen, *The Journal for the Scientific Study of
   Religion*, Vol. IV, No. 2 (April, 1965), pp. 145-151. Jacque
   Ellul, *The New Demons*, trans. C. Edward Hopkins, (New York: The
   Seabury Press, 1975).

2. *Islam Observed; Religious Development in Morocco and Indonesia*,
   Clifford Geertz (New Haven: Yale University Press, 1968), pp.
   96-97. Geertz's essays, "Thick Description: Towards and Interpretive Theory of Culture" and, "Religion As a Cultural System"
   brought together in *The Interpretation of Cultures*, (New York:
   Basic Books, 1973) elaborate on this suggestion.

3. The theme of homelessness in its modern sense has preoccupied
   artists and intellectuals since the last century. Peter Berger
   has highlighted it in his thorough analysis, *The Homeless Mind,
   Modernization and Consciousness*, (New York: Random House, 1973).

4. *The Human Condition*, Hannah Arendt (Chicago: The University of
   Chicago, 1958), pp. 253-254.

5. See Owen Barfield's, *Saving the Appearances, A Study in Idolatry*,
   (London: Faber and Faber, 1962). The work of Michael Polanyi
   analyzes a number of these factors.

6. *Prosperity Follows Settlement in Western Canada*, Issued under the
   direction of Hon. Frank Oliver, Minister of the Interior (Ottawa:
   Canadian Government Print, 1905).

7. *To Canada*, Published by the authority of Hon. Clifford Sifton,
   Minister of the Interior (Ottawa: Canadian Government Print,
   1903).

8. H. Richard Niebuhr, *The Social Sources of Denominationalism* (New
   York: The New American Library, 1975), p. 200.

9. "The Perpetuation of the Muslim Tradition in the Canadian North,"
   Harold Barkley, *The Muslim World*, Vol. LIX (January, 1969), pp.
   64-72.

10. H. Richard Niebhur, *op. cit.*, p. 204.

11. The place and function of revivalism in the frontier setting was
    initially discussed in the work of William Warren Sweet, "The
    Frontier in American Christianity," *Environmental Factors in
    Christian History*, ed. J. T. McNeil, *et al.*, (Chicago: University

of Chicago, 1939) and "The Church as Moral Courts of the Frontier," *Church History*, Vol. 11, No. 1 (March, 1933) pp. 3-21.
Also see Merrill E. Gaddis, "Religious Ideas and Attitudes in
the Early Frontier," *Church History*, Vol. 11, No. 1 (March, 1933)
pp. 152-170. Jerald C. Brauer in "Changing Perspectives on Religion in America" has some illuminating thoughts on revivalism as
rite of passage on the frontier, *Reinterpretation in American
Church History*, ed. Jerald C. Brauer (Chicago: University of
Chicago, 1968) pp. 1-28. The Canadian situation is treated in a
preliminary fashion in John T. McNeils "Religious and Moral Conditions Among the Canadian Pioneers," *The American Society of
Church History Papers*, Second Series, Vol. 8, (1928), pp. 67-122.

12. H. Richard Niebhur, *op. cit.*, p. 206.

13. The author's field notes (Spring, 1975).

14. "Hutterite Worship and Preaching," Robert Friedmann, *The Mennonite
Quarterly Review*, Vol. XL, No. 1 (January, 1966), pp. 5-25.

15. Robert Friedman, *op. cit.*, p. 11.

16. The author's field notes (Fall, 1975).

17. I have not had the opportunity as yet to visit the colony where
the photocopy machine presumably exists.

18. The following titles are published under the Mercury Series im-
print for the Canadian Center for Folk Culture Studies, National
Museum of Man, Ottawa, Canada. *Norwegian Settlers in Alberta*,
Jan Harold Brunvard (1974). *The Swedish Community at Eriksdale*,
George J. Houser (1976). *Japanese Folk Culture in Alberta*, Carlo
Caldarola (prepared in 1976 and read in manuscript form. To be
published.) *Folk Culture of Sikhs and Hindus in Alberta*, Jennifer
K. Bowerman (prepared in 1976 and read in manuscript form. To be
published.) *Danish Settlements on the Canadian Prairies: Folk
Traditions, Immigrant Experience, and Local History*, Frank M.
Paulsen (1974).

THE MENNONITE EXPERIENCE IN CANADA

"I'm asking whether the use of a name which has an ethnic connotation (as Mennonite Brethren) should not be reconsidered. [On the other hand can we] retain our spiritual heritage [if we drop the name?] ...It is the biggest issue we have faced in 50 years"--F. C. Peters (Mennonite Brethren Moderator, quoted in *MB Herald*, July 22, 1977).

Introduction

In the 1971 Census of Canada, as in every previous census, the Mennonites are classified as a religious group, but, like the Jews, they could qualify for listing in both religious and ethnic categories. While most Mennonites see themselves as a religious people, they have, for the most part, acquired a character than can unquestionably be defined in ethnic terms. This development is in part due to their theology and religious practices, to governmental pressures, to the sociologies of their communities, and to the psychologies arising from all of these.

It is hazardous to generalize, however, because Mennonites are a heterogeneous group. There are many paradoxes and contradictions. Different historic experiences arising from their many migrations and settlement patterns, different degrees of isolation and accommodation, and diverse approaches to religious nurture and renewal have produced many minorities within the Mennonite minority. This means that the conclusions to be drawn from the Mennonite religious and ethnic experience in Canada may also be multiple.

An oversimplified but useful approach to the Canadian Mennonites is to see them as two cultural families with separate European origins and migrations to the new world. On the one hand, we have those from Switzerland and southern German states, who, beginning in 1786, came to Upper Canada from Pennsylvania where they arrived from Europe beginning a century earlier. In this essay they will be referred to as the Swiss Mennonites or simply as the Swiss. It should be kept in mind that this designation will usually also include the Amish, a distinct Mennonite branch in the Swiss Mennonite cultural family.

On the other hand, are the Mennonites of Dutch-North German origins, who arrived in Canada in several major and numerous minor migrations beginning in 1874. Their European wanderings had taken them

eastward to Prussia in the sixteenth century and to Russia late in the
eighteenth.   In this essay this group of Mennonites will be known as
the Dutch, a designation admittedly debatable because of duality in
the cultural history of these people.

Both the Swiss and the Dutch experienced a transformation in the
sense of becoming ethnic though not quite in the same way and with the
same effect.   Yet, they had in common a wholistic notion of religion,
common beliefs and practices, and a communal approach to life.

The inevitable result was an almost complete overlapping of the
two spheres, religion and ethnicity.   Religion tended to take on an
ethnic character and ethnicity became thoroughly infused with the features of religion.   The relationship had paradoxical effects, contri-
buting at one and the same time to creativity and to sterility, as well
as to solidity and fluidity in their communities.   All of this and much
more will be illustrated in the historic review and analysis to follow.

1.   Radical Breaks and Beginnings

The Mennonite experience in Canada cannot be understood apart from
the origins in Europe, which saw radical breaks in religious and cultural continuity and new beginnings in both areas.   First known as
Anabaptists or rebaptizers, the Mennonites belonged to the so-called
religious left-wing of the Reformation.   At the heart of their dissent
was the notion that religious commitment and community could come only
with a voluntary discipleship at a mature age.   This required the rejection of infant baptism, a universally recognized religious ritual,
with social and political import in the Holy Roman Empire so significant that the civic authorities became the guardians of a society sup-
posedly Christian.

Other radical ideas had to do with the rejection of state authority over the religious conscience and of ecclesiastical authority when
it came to interpreting the Bible.   Every believer was perceived to be
a priest, capable of discerning and interpreting the mind of God.
Both, the oath, as a symbol of an ultimate earthly allegiance, and the
sword, as an instrument of ultimate power, were rejected as not belonging to those whose primary loyalty was the kingdom of God and
whose primary citizenship was the disciplined community of believers
which symbolized that kingdom.

The social effect of this new religious stance was discontinuity
with the existing society in almost every sphere of life.   The fires
of prolonged persecution completed the separation begun by the

ostracization that accompanies any challenge to established political
and religious norms and strongly entrenched cultural habits. As the
Anabaptists were separated from society, voluntarily and involuntarily,
they were also separated from a given culture. Not only were they
driven from the cities and villages into the hills, the woods, and
river valleys, but they were read out of the society of their day in
every way.

They survived only because of new communities which they formed
in rural hideouts and on the fringes of the empire where independent-
minded nobles were sympathetic to their protest. Mennonites did not
form communities as complete as did their Anabaptist cousins, the
communistic Hutterites, but they too approached total community, because of their wholistic theology. The common religious beliefs and
ordinances, the common political fate, the common flight from persecution, the common struggle for existence, and the common leadership,
all contributed to the emergence of a new culture.

Thus, while Mennonite theology of dissent from an old way of life
broke and destroyed one culture, Mennonite theology of assent to a new
way of life soon established a new culture. In their new congregational communities the high priority given to children, to continuity
of family life, to social discipline, and to a value system that embraced all of life, the Mennonites gradually shaped an integrated culture which, on the one hand, could be called religion, and, on the
other hand, ethnicity, assuming broad definitions for both.

2. Holy Experiment and Religious Commonwealth

The fusion of the religious and ethnic elements in the Mennonite
experience reached their zenith in those American and Russian environments which immediately preceded and which profoundly affected the
Mennonite experience in Canada. It happened when the Swiss became part
of Wm. Penn's "holy experiment" in Pennsylvania beginning in 1683 and
when the Dutch created a "commonwealth" in south Russia beginning a
century later in 1789. In both, the Mennonite evolution came full
circle. In both situations Mennonites became known by themselves as
well as by others not only by their baptism as adults and Mennonite
church membership but also by their birth into Mennonite families.

There were important differences, however, between the two histories. Penn's holy experiment was not only for Mennonites but for
other pacifistic groups like the Quakers of which he was one. Indeed,
religious sectarians and dissenters of all kinds found refuge in this

new political kingdom of tolerance, peace, and love. In Pennsylvania
they found the three things most essential to their happy development,
at least for several generations: an abundance of good land, a fair
measure of political freedom, and both of these in the context of the
Germanic homeland culture. This culture underwent a transformation
sufficient to become known as the Pennsylvania Dutch (meaning Deutsch
or German) culture. The main ingredients of this culture was a peculiar German dialect, most communicative in social discourse and capable
of absorbing anglicizations. However, associated with the culture was
not only a language but in due course also all those skills and crafts
which sprang from a creative agricultural community and a domestic enterprise, which saw practically all the food, clothing, shelter, and
furniture provided from within the extended family. The cultural at-
tributes ranged all the way from fraktur art and fancy quilts to unique
styles in house construction and the manufacture of implements.

While the Mennonites were a part of this cultural development,
they were not the only ones. Thus, Pennsylvania set the stage for an
ethnicity, which belonged to the Mennonites and identified them, but
not exclusively. The ethnic identity, therefore, was larger than
Mennonite, with a two-fold effect upon them. On the one hand, the
broader ethnicity became the vehicle of understanding, tolerance, and
ecumenical feeling, as well as a context for social assimilation and
the absorption of new religious ideas.

On the other hand, the trend to socialization and assimilation
produced a "backlash" among those who were not about to have Mennonite
values and identity swallowed up entirely, either in evangelical revivalism or in a broadly-defined social culture, be this Pennsylvania
Dutch or Anglo-American. The defence mechanism which facilitated resistance was the more narrow and rigid prescription of those cultural
traits which were deemed essential to the preservation of religious
values. This religious conservatism in turn became a cultural conservatism, which signaled not only a longer life for the Pennsylvania
Dutch culture in general but for a unique Mennonite ethnicity in particular.

Back in Europe, Mennonites were not the only German colonists to
accept the invitation of Catherine II to become agricultural pioneers
in New Russia--there were many German Catholics and German Lutherans
as well. Yet, so separate and autonomous were the Mennonite colonies
that one can speak of the emergence in Russia of a Mennonite commonwealth as well as of a distinct Mennonite culture. Land was deeded to

the Mennonites as a people for their exclusive use. Schools, roads, and civic affairs became their responsibility in the colonies of Chortitz and Molotschna, which together embraced about a 100 villages and which soon gave birth to daughter colonies of a similar nature.

In these colonies the ecclesiastical and governmental authorities became so intertwined that the Mennonite areas became states within a state, thus reproducing in miniature the features of the Holy Roman Empire against which their Anabaptist forefathers had once rebelled. Mennonite took on a double meaning. On the one hand it meant church membership, initiated by baptism. On the other hand, it meant from the time of birth citizenship in a community.

In South Russia the use of the High German language, which already in Prussia had replaced the Dutch as the language of worship and education, was reinforced, while the Low German dialect, used in social intercourse and business, became, like Pennsylvania Dutch, a vehicle for linguistic adjustment through the absorption of Russian words. Generally speaking, however, there was only minimal adaptation. The experience of the Mennonite cultural island, surrounded by the waters of a Slavic sea, had the effect of isolation and of the development of a very distinctive Mennonite ethnicity and, moreover of feelings of racial superiority, all in the context of values that continued to be expressed in religious terms.

3. Swiss and Dutch Transplants

As already reported, the Mennonites eventually made their way to Canada, the Swiss from Pennsylvania and Europe (referring to the Amish) after the American and French revolutions, respectively. The Dutch-German Mennonites came from Russia, after a mini-revolution in that country, which began the freeing of the serfs, the democratization of the military, and the russification of the minorities.

The Swiss came to Ontario, where they assumed settlement patterns in accordance with their social orientation. Those, with assimilationist tendencies already established, were satisfied with good land, good neighbours, and good churches. The churches did not have to be Mennonite nor did the neighbours, though a distinct preference was shown for Pennsylvania Dutch communities. Those whose religious symbols and values were preferably Mennonite sought to settle on lands contiguous to acreages already settled by other Mennonites. Greatly facilitating such settlement were the German Land Company, which

bought and sold land for those coming from Pennsylvania, and the setting aside of the so-called German Block for the Amish coming from
Europe.

These relatively solid Mennonite settlements in Waterloo County
did not, however, settle for all time the question of Mennonite identity and destiny. Each situation and each generation knew differen-
tiation when it came to choosing different degrees of isolation and
different degrees or kinds of assimilation. The matter was never settled for all time, partly because every successive time of tension produced clearer lines of conflict and choice. In the end, an old order
orientation became isolationist in the extreme, while a new order orientation tended toward assimilation in the extreme. Most Mennonites
usually found themselves somewhere between the two extremes. Be that
as it may, assimilation sometimes meant adjustment of cultural forms
and languages, sometimes also the surrender of values.

The Dutch who arrived from Russia in the 1870s settled in Manitoba
on blocks of land, known as East and West (of the Red River) Reserves,
and negotiated as their exclusive domain prior to immigration. The
choice of Canada and Manitoba were very deliberate because it seemed
most likely that the Mennonite commonwealth could be perpetuated in
that environment. Block settlement, the village system, parochial
schools, and other forms of self-government were impossible in America
where many other Mennonite immigrants went, and their unhampered development seemed to be threatened also in Russia.

In other words, the most desirable form of community life, influenced, if not dominated, in all of its aspects by religion, was to be
pursued on the Manitoba reserves, and on similar ones established
after a while in Saskatchewan. And this pursuit was successful to a
very large extent, at least for a generation. After the difficult
pioneering years, a prosperous agricultural economy, well laid-out
villages and gardens, a comprehensive private school system, and large
families guaranteed the continuation of the Mennonite commonwealth.

In due course the coming of municipal government, public schools,
railroads, and business, and the ending of reserve status also brought
to an end to the commonwealth in its ideal form, but not to religion
and ethnicity, now an indisputable fact of Mennonite existence. Like
the Ukrainians and the French, so the Mennonites in southern Manitoba
were known as a distinct ethnic group.

4. Religious Renewal and Reform

In due course, and before the end of the nineteenth century, religious restlessness appeared in both settlement communities, among
the Swiss in Ontario and among the Dutch in Manitoba. This restlessness was stirred by internal feelings that all was not well with the
House of Menno and by external influences, which became the measuring
stick of religious well-being and the guide to how things could be improved. These influences were in the main revivalism and denominationalism. Revivalism, allied with the Sunday School, challenged both the
style and content of Mennonite religious nurture. Denominationalism
suggested a new form of organization, which was oriented toward programs and budgets rather than the life of the community.

Both influences appealed to those Mennonites who viewed the quiet,
non-professional, and traditional forms, led by lay preachers and
bishops, as sterile, and not sufficiently attractive for the young
people, not to speak of outsiders. The same Mennonites tended to view
their communities as too parochial, too ethnicity-bound, too closed to
outsiders. What was needed was the use of the English language in
preaching, four-part singing, Sunday schools, mission programs, budgets, evangelistic revivals, use of pianos, cathedral-style churches,
and above all better organization with non-ordained members in church
councils and constitutions curbing the power of the bishops. Greater
participation in public affairs and in the business community was assumed to be necessary and desirable.

In Ontario as well as Manitoba the restlessness led to breaks in
the Mennonite church communities, with the new order of things championed by the new groups which carried such names as Mennonite Brethren in Christ among the Swiss, and Mennonite Brethren and Evangelical
Mennonite Brethren among the Dutch. Perhaps the main result everywhere
was the growth of individualism at the expense of the traditional community. Personal conversions, private enterprise, and independent congregations, all tended to flow together as features of the new culture.
As has been written elsewhere:

> ...in the period from 1870 to 1910, the Brethren
> had accepted six major innovations: the Sunday
> school, revivalism, a church periodical, a formal
> missionary program, Wesleyan holiness and a
> church-sponsored educational institution. These
> six innovations had a profound effect upon the
> denomination's concept of the church. The early
> idea of the separated community, an obedient and
> faithful social organism, was to a large degree

> replaced by an individualistic understanding of
> the faith concerned primarily with a salvation
> that was personalized, an ethic that was inter-
> nalized, and a community that was millennialized
> or postponed (Epp. *Mennonites in Canada*, p. 263).

While the above commentary refers to events in the late nineteenth
century, the influences of revivalism broke out with similar effects
repeatedly in the twentieth century. The forces of an individualistic
evangelicalism, originating largely in the USA, may have done more than
the Canadian environment to shape the Mennonite character in the latter
part of the century.

The attractions of evangelicalism lay in its emphasis on bibli-
cism, a traditional Mennonite value, on the one hand, and its allowance
for a respectable assimilation, on the on the other hand. On the surface it seemed that evangelicalism brought Mennonites back to their
Anabaptist roots, meaning individual faith, purity, and zeal. In the
long run, however, its effects in undermining wholeness, the Anabaptist
ethic, and an ethnicity, which was an essential social glue, could not
be denied. As one bishop of an evangelicized denomination said to a
leader in a group still thoroughly ethnic: "It's easier for us to get
people to join us, but it's also much easier for us to lose them. We
know what it takes to convert them, but we have no real community that
keeps them."

Actually, each religious group needs a cultural framework since
the human community abhors an ethnic vacuum. Evangelicalism had the
effect of exchanging the culture of ethnicity for the culture of nationalism, also among the Mennonites.

5. Public Education and Patriotism

An equally serious threat to the Mennonite way of life--religion
with a communal and ethnic base--came in the early nineteenth century
with attempts to shape the Canadian dominion as a reliable, loyal, and
patriotic component of the British Empire. The public school became
one of the main vehicles of anglicization and the inculcation of patriotic values. Its thrust was felt most in Manitoba and Saskatchewan, to
a lesser extent in Ontario.

In Ontario, the Swiss Mennonites had long ago adjusted to so-called public schools, partly because they had been the founders, partly
because the religious element in the public school curriculum was one
of the foundations of the province. The Swiss battle with the public
system would come at a later time. In Manitoba, on the other hand, the
province had done a major battle with church-based education at the

close of the nineteenth century in order to achieve a single, unilin-
gual, more adequate, consequently public, system for the province.

While the target had been the French Catholic schools, the Mennonites had not been spared because their schools, largely German, were
limited in their curriculum, and not ranking very high in terms of prevailing educational standards and teacher training. In both provinces,
Manitoba and Saskatchewan, the so-called conservative Mennonites were
determined to maintain their schools, not only because this had been
one of the conditions of emigration to Canada but because the public
schools were a threat to all they held dear: religious values, a
separate culture and way of life, and, last but not least, non-partici-
pation in war or even in flag worship and other national idolatries.

The war itself confronted the Mennonites with certain dilemmas,
chief of which was the redefinition and interpreation of who they were.
Officially, and ideally, Mennonites were persons who were baptized
members of the church. It so happened, however, that the military con-
scription age was several years ahead of the normal baptismal age.
The war came to a conclusion before ultimate tests could be applied,
but it had become obvious that the Mennonites felt compelled to define
as Mennonites all those who were part of the community, thus confirming
the ethnic definition. To at least some extent, this self-understanding conformed to official Canadian perceptions. In 1873 the Dominion
Government had recognized this definition, and the Census of Canada had
from the beginning included Mennonite children in the decennial count
of Canadians.

Be that as it may, the war and the public schools represented a
turning point for Canada and the Mennonites. Both knew that the status
of religious and ethnic minorities had changed. Mennonite reaction was
of three kinds: unquestioning acceptance and assimilation, making the
best of it through strengthened institutions of their own, or migrating
to other countries. In the 1920s thousands of Mennonites, having concluded that survival in Canada was impossible, found new homes and new
autonomy in Mexico and in Paraguay.

6.   The Coming of the Russlaeuder

If the war brought profound changes to the Canadian Mennonite
scene, so did the immigration which followed it. The largest successful mass Mennonite movement in history brought 20,000 emigres of the
Russian revolution to Canada, even while the descendants of their pre-
decessors to this country were migrating to Latin America. The Russian

Mennonites of the 1920s were different from those of the 1870s in a
number of ways. Their freedom in Russia had in the intervening years
not been curtailed to the expected extent. On the contrary, between
1874 and 1914 the commonwealth had in some ways been perfected with
the help of economic prosperity, a vast system of schools, improved
ecclesiastical organization and leadership, and sophistication in culture, including the production of literature.

All this they brought with them, and though their settlements were
scattered from ONtario to British Columbia before World War II, they
found ways of tying them all together in various cultural and ecclesiastical organizations. Most remarkable was their advancement of provincial and national organizations and the establishment of educational
institutions. Music fests, youth activities, literary evenings, teacher training institutes, theatrical events, and, most importantly, special Saturday schools to preserve the German language, all became part
of their cultural thrusts.

The promotion of the German language proceeded so vigorously that
the Germanism of some Mennonites flowed together with the pan-Germanism
of Third Reich propaganda. Indeed, some even became enamoured with Na
Nazi theories of race and with Hitler's political program generally.
While all of this helped in the 1930s to advance the Mennonite culture
as something distinct, resisting anglicization in Canada as russification had been resisted in Russia, it did produce its own backlash.

When the war broke out, the sons of the immigrants had great difficulty reconciling a zealous Germanism, even if only at the cultural
level, with a responsible citizenship. Thus the war reversed the directions of Mennonite culture and threatened traditional Mennonite
ethnicity. More significantly, the reaction against Mennonite religious values, especially conscientious objection to war. Germanism
and opposition to war were seen by some as an inseparable ethno-reli-
gious package in the same way that anglicization, patriotism, and mili-
tarism seemed to go hand in hand.

7. Aftermath of World War II

The immediate consequences for the Mennonites of World War II
were several, including additional immigrations and emigrations, further assimilationist trends, and new efforts to save Mennonitism through
the building of institutions.

Once again Russian and Prussian Mennonite refugees and displaced
persons by the thousands arrived from Europe, either directly or via

Latin America. This had the effect of strengthening the German language and holding up significant transition to the English for at
least a decade. On the other hand, since most of the immigrants settled in the cities, the process of urbanization was speeded up.

All of the forces set in motion by World War II--cultural transition, patriotism, urbanization--persuaded some Mennonites that Canada
was no place to be if cherished values were to be preserved for suc-
ceeding generations. As after the Great War, so now too additional
emigrations took place, including a small one of several hundred to
Mexico and a larger one of several thousand to Paraguay. The total on-
slaught of Canadian society on minority groups, including once again
the impact of the public school and the mass media, as a force relatively new, contributed significantly to the fears that a satisfactory
future in Canada could not be found.

Assimilationist trends, apart from the urbanization already noted,
were in two directions, both with strong religious overtones. On the
one hand, were those Mennonites with an evangelical orientation, whose
embarrassment with Mennonite ethnicity and Mennonite objection to participation in wars, had become unbearable. An entire denominational
group, which had been moving away from the Mennonite centre ever since
championing the new order in the nineteenth century, decided in 1947
to drop the Mennonite name. This option would be considered by others
in the years to come. Returned "Mennonite" soldiers, on the other
hand, became the base for new congregations of the United Church, the
Lutheran Church, or similar churches of more liberal identification.
Though some veterans found their way back into the Mennonite congregations most were unwanted, or felt unwanted, because the incompatibility
of soldiering and Mennonite church membership was still a strong tradition.

The war also unleashed new determination and energy to strengthen
Mennonitism through institutions. At least seven private Mennonite
high schools, numberous Bible schools, and several colleges were founded in the 1940s or early 1950s. Youth organizations were strengthened
and youth periodicals were begun. Sometimes the institutions founded
assumed different directions for the Mennonites. Thus, we have, on the
one hand, the founding of the Society for the Preservation of the German Language, and, on the other hand, the founding of a national, in-
ter-Mennonite, English language weekly newspaper, which symbolized the
post-war language transition among the Dutch. The Swiss, for the most
part, had made the switch before and after World War I.

8. Three Paths to Survival

The several paths pointing to Mennonite survival and to a satisfactory identity in the three decades since the War can be summarized
with the words colony, conference, and culture. Though the three approaches could not be totally separated from each other--to various
degrees they appeared combined at various times in various situations--
they were accented by some Mennonite groups and individuals more than
by others.

The idea of the colony was related to land, agricultural settlement, and Mennonitism as a total way of life. Colonies, in the sense
of the Commonwealth (as in Russia), or German Tracts and Blocks (as in
Ontario), or Reserves (as in Manitoba) were no longer possible in Canada. To satisfy the urge to perpetuate the Mennonite colony two approaches were taken. On the one hand there were additional migrations
to foreign countries like Bolivia where colonies could still be set up.

On the other hand, there was still a Canadian frontier to be con-
quered in the northern regions of Alberta and British Columbia. The
Swiss in Ontario, including new Old Order Amish from the United States,
satisfied the needs of a community-based agricultural Mennonitism, by
settling as far away from urban areas as was practical and by forming
neighborhoods as tightly-knit as possible. The latter was necessary
also to accommodate horse-drawn transportation and small one-room private schools, which were introduced in the 1960s. By that time the
coming of large impersonal school systems had persuaded the old order
Swiss that Mennonite values and ways were threatened by these systems.
Generally speaking, the "Colony Mennonites" were most successful in
preserving Mennonite values and ethnicity.

By far the largest grouping of Mennonites could be called "Conference Mennonites." Actually, there were about ten conference families in Canada in each of the Swiss and Dutch traditions. Conferences
borrowed heavily from Protestant denominationalism, generally speaking.
Conferences were the ecclesiastical equivalent of, or substitute for,
the commonwealth or colony idea. They tied together widely dispersed
congregations, in rural and urban areas, most with memberships of less
than 100 (though a few had 500 or more, especially in urban centres).
Conferences were the umbrella for, and provided the funding of, institutions. Conferences gave identity and familial feeling. Their
"territory" was not land but institutions.

A third orientation had to do with culture. The "Culture Mennonites" had some commonality with Colony Mennonites in that they

resisted the narrow definition of religion which came with the Conferences. The commonality with Conference Mennonites lay in the fact
that both were without land and both depended heavily on institutions
and events.

Cultural activity had two thrusts. On the one hand, were those
who wanted to preserve the German language and German ethnicity at all
costs. On the other hand, were those who had accepted a language transition but who wanted the richest possible expression of Mennonitism
in the English language. The latter was greatly facilitated by historic anniversaries which came in the 1970s, and which got their cue in
part from the Canadian centennial in 1967. These historic events included:

- in 1972 the sesquicentennial of Amish immigration;
- in 1973 the 50th and 25th anniversaries of the second and third
  immigrations from Russia;
- in 1974 the centennial of Mennonite immigration from Russia;
- in 1975 the 450th anniversary of Anabaptism;
- in 1976 the 200th anniversary of the American revolution which
  helped to bring the first Mennonites to Canada.

Drama, films, concerts, fests of all kinds, and an abundance of
literature reinforced the cultural dimension of Mennonite life and its
ethnicity in the wider sense.

9. Multiculturalism and Minorities

All of the above was greatly encouraged by a new climate of multiculturalism, promoted and to a great extent funded by both provincial and federal governments. Minority cultures, religious dissent,
and ethnic identity were now assets, and not liabilities, as they had
been for such a long period in history. The writing of histories, the
founding of archives, and the taping of memoirs greatly enhanced Mennonite feeling and self-understanding.

Multiculturalism, however, was too recent to allow the conclusion
that a favourable climate for Mennonite religion and ethnicity would
enhance it at the deeper levels and contribute to its survival in the
long run. A case could be made for multiculturalism being another name
for the melting pot of a new, less monolithic, Canadianism, a fine way
to get all minorities really to become Canadian in a sense acceptable
to them and allowable in peactime by a tolerant, perhaps complacent,
Canadian populace.

Multiculturalism and minority rights were by no means guaranteed, however. Working against constitutions and official policies were the levelling effects and conformist pressures of mass society, mass education, mass media, mass religion, and mass politics. Additionally, the technocratic society was computerizing all of life, making it exceedingly difficult for old order Amish and old order Mennonites to resist modernization. Lower level bureaucrats too did not know the meanings of multiculturalism and minority rights when translated into administrative procedures.

Finally, Canada's immigration policies and the growth of a multiracial society had the potential for producing a backlash against multiculturalism. It was not yet clear that Canada understood multiculturalism to mean or imply multiracialism. Until multiracialism was fully accepted or until multiculturalism had been tested in a time of war or other national crisis, it could not be assumed that minority rights and the tolerance of ethnicity in the deepest sense had been accepted as indispensable values by most Canadians.

10. Some Hypotheses and Theories

From the Mennonite experience various relationships between religion and ethnicity can be suggested as follows:

- Radical religious experience can bring about ethnic discontinuity.
- Religion, broadly defined, and ethnicity, broadly defined, have much in common; sometimes there is complete overlap.
- Religion and ethnicity, both narrowly and rigidly defined, tend to militate against each other in the sense that they exclude each other.
- A holistic religion tends to create and foster ethnicity.
- Religion abhors a cultural vacuum and if religious renewal discards one form of ethnicity it will tend to adopt another.
- Religious and cultural or ethnic conservatism (in the sense of preservation) tend to go hand in hand.
- Ethnicity's effect on religion can be creativity or sterility, and the reverse is also true.
- Ethnicity, as a positive force, makes for a close religious community, and, as, a negative force, it tends toward a closed religious community.
- Sound religion and wholesome ethnicity are impossible without each other.

- The religious and political environment can have a profound effect on the religion and ethnicity of minority groups.
- Institutions, such as public or private schools, do much to strengthen or weaken the religious and ethnic qualities of minority groups.

National events, such as wars, and national phenomena, such as urbanization or multiculturalism, have a very significant effect on minority groups who have opposed war, been rural in their life style, or not enjoyed a favourable cultural climate in the past.

Conclusion

All of the above is only an introduction to the subject of religion and ethnicity in the Canadian Mennonite experience. But it probably is sufficient to illustrate that further study would be not only highly interesting but exceedingly useful in understanding the dynamics of minority religious and ethnic groups in a pluralistic society which hopes to survive as a single nation.

SELECT BIBLIOGRAPHY

Driedger, Leo. "In Search of Identity Factors: A Comparison of Eth-
    nic Minorities in Manitoba," *Canadian Review of Sociology and
    Anthropology*, May, 1975.

Driedger, Leo. "Urbanization of Mennonites in Canada," *Call to Faith-
    fulness: Essays in Canadian Mennonite Studies*, Rudy Regehr (ed.),
    Winnipeg, Manitoba: Canadian Mennonite Bible College, 1972.

Dyck, Cornelius J. *Introduction to Mennonite History: A Popular His-
    tory of the Anabaptists and the Mennonites*. Scottdale, Pa.:
    Herald Press, 1967.

Epp, Frank H. *Mennonite Exodus: The Rescue and Resettlement of the
    Russian Mennonites Since the Communist Revolution*. Altona, Mani-
    toba: D. W. Friesen & Sons Ltd., 1962.

Epp, Frank H. *Mennonites in Canada, 1786-1920: The History of a Sep-
    arate People*. Toronto: Macmillan of Canada, 1974.

Epp, Frank H. *Mennonite Peoplehood: A Plea for New Initiatives*.
    Waterloo, Ont.: Conrad Press, 1977.

Epp, Frank H. "An Analysis of Germanism and National Socialism in the
    Immigrant Newspapers of a Canadian Minority Group, The Mennonites,
    in the 1930s." Unpublished Ph.D. Dissertation, University of
    Minnesota, 1965 (Microfilm #66-1660).

Francis, E. K. *In Search of Utopia: The Mennonites in Manitoba*.
    Altona, Manitoba: D. W. Friesen & Sons Ltd., 1955.

Fretz, J. Winfield. *Pilgrims in Paraguay: The Story of Mennonite
    Colonization in South America*. Scottdale, Pa.: Herald Press,
    1953.

Klaassen, Walter. *Anabaptism: Neither Catholic nor Protestant*.
    Waterloo, Ont.: Conrad Press, 1973.

Redekop, Calvin W. *The Old Colony Mennonites: Dilemmas of Ethnic
    Minority Life*. Baltimore: John Hopkins Press, 1969.

Sawatzky, Harry Leonard. *They Sought a Country: Mennonite Coloniza-
    tion in Mexico. With an Appendix on Mennonite Colonization in
    British Honduras*. Berkeley: University of California, 1971.

Smucker, Don E. Bibliography on Mennonites and Hutterites to be pub-
    lished in 1977 (October) by Wilfrid Laurier University, Waterloo,
    Ontario.

CHANGES IN THE JAPANESE TRUE PURE LAND BUDDHISM IN ALBERTA
- A Case Study: Honpa Buddhist Church in Alberta -

The history and development of the Buddhist movement in Southern
Alberta has been closely tied to the settling of the Japanese as a
minority group in Canada. Buddhism, more accurately the Japanese True
Pure Land School Buddhism, came to Canada and to Southern Alberta when
the Japanese migrated to Canada in search of a new frontier. As a
consequence, the problem which the Japanese faced in their new adven-
ture reflected, to some degree, the problems which the Japanese Pure
Land Buddhism faced in its developmental phases of secularization and
assimilation.

This paper will highlight the historical and liturgical background in which the Japanese Pure Land Buddhism developed and was nurtured; the manner in which it was established as a School of Japanese
Buddhism; its transference to Canada by people who were molded by the
Meiji and Taishō periods of Japanese history; the changes it underwent,
and is still undergoing, to become assimilated into the Canadian culture; and some hypotheses concerning the future.

I. The Historical and Liturgical Background
The Jōdo-shin-shu (True Pure Land School) is a unique form of
Japanese Buddhism said to be founded by Shinran (1173-1262). It differs fundamentally from other Buddhist schools in that, whereas the
others make a distinction between a monk and a layman, the True Pure
Land School does not. An analysis of the changes in the interpretation of the term *saṅgha* that took place during the spread of Buddhism
from India to Japan will help clarify matters. In India, the term
saṅgha referred to a gathering of monks and nuns and only by extension
did it include the laity. In China and in Japan, especially with the
development of the *Jōdo-shu* (Pure Land School), the congregation comprised both monks and laymen. It was Shinran, who emphasized the
fact that enlightenment was not limited to monks, nuns, and ascetics,
but that the Buddha's teaching was meant for all walks of life.

Shinran began his religious quest at a very early age. Moved by
the sudden and early death of both his parents, he sought refuge in
the *Buddha-dharma*. He studied and practiced the Buddhist way of Mt.

Hiei[1], the centre for the Japanese Tendai School. Tradition states
that at one time while Shinran was making his pilgrimages to various
temples throughout Kyoto, he stopped at a temple called *Rokkaku-do*.
There he meditated for one hundred days during which time Shōtoku
Taishi (574-622), the Prince Regent who declared Buddhism as an official religion of Japan in his *Constitution of Seventeen Articles*, was
said to have appeared in the form of a vision. It is said that due to
the vision, Shinran abandoned his priestly life to take up the path of
an ordinary person, but there is no textual basis for this theory. In
any event, that Shinran did give up his priestly life is evident in
view of the fact that he took the step of marriage. Contrary to the
life style of a monk for whom celibacy was the custom, Shinran's marriage to Eshinni was revolutionary.

Shinran's religious commitment can be summarized with the term
Nembutsu (recitation of the Buddha's name). Shinran was introduced to
the *Nembutsu* by Genku, or Hōnen (1133-1212) as he is better known.
According to Hōnen, the *Nembutsu* practice was an act by which the re-
citer accumulated merits whereby an enlightened state could be attained. In the Pure Land School, this enlightened state was called *Jōdo*
(Pure Land) which could be attained upon one's death. As time went on
controversies arose within the Pure Land School as to whether one recitation with a sincere mind was not worth more than a hundred recitations by one who lacked sincerity. It was Shinran who gave a new
interpretation by advocating that the *Nembutsu* had nothing to do with
the accumulation of merits nor did the numbers of recitation have any
significance. He advocated that the *Nembutsu* was an expression of
gratitude.

In Shinran's view, "gratitude" meant a feeling of joy in having
gained human existence; a sincereity of mind which enabled one to live
a life of decorum; and a desire to become enlightened which meant to
listen to the Buddha's teachings with earnestness. Shinran claimed
that gratitude could not be gained by one's efforts alone. For Shinran, joy, sincerity, and the desire to become enlightened were actual-
ized through the workings of causes and circumstances; thus, the feeling of gratitude was a spontaneous outcome when one became aware of
his indebtedness to the causes and conditions which made life possible.
Gratitude was not something one could impose upon himself; it resulted
from an interaction with the "other".

The presence of the term "other power" has caused many to confuse the teaching of the True Pure Land School with Christian doctrines, especially the doctrine of grace. The reason for the confusion may stem from the fact that the English language itself presents a problem. That is, it is the nature of a language to reflect its own limitations. For instance, in contrast, when one reads a Japanese translation of the Bible, one finds that it is loaded with words which give it a Chinese Confucian or Japanese Shinto flavour. However, just as any adherent of the Bible will attest, and a reading of it in English will clarify, a Japanese translation of the Bible, to be understood properly, cannot be read by interpreting the words which appear therein in a Chinese Confucian or Japanese Shinto sense. Even though words are "borrowed" from a Japanese culture context, they must be understood in a "Christian" sense. This requires the added task of edification and interpretation. The same can be said about an English translation of a Buddhist text. One simply cannot expect to approach it as if he were reading a book by Carl Barth. Thus, when the term "other power" is translated by the word "grace", one must not be too hasty to come to a Biblical conclusion, as did the translators who were themselves of a Biblical tradition or who, if they were not, tried to "modernize" the Buddhist texts. When interpreting the term "grace" as a translation of what in a True Pure Land Buddhism context means "other power," one must not lose sight of the fundamental Buddhist principle, concisely stated in the *Āryapratītyasamutpādasutra* as follows:

> The cause of those things produced from causes has been told by the Tathāgata. So also their extinction is spoken about by the great ascetic.[2]

In other words, "grace" in a True Pure Land Buddhism context refers to the principle of co-arising and co-extinction (*pratītyasamutpāda*).

The *Nembutsu* practice advocated by Shinran gained popularity among the masses. His method was simple and even refreshing for those who lived at a time and in a society filled with uncertainties. Literary works, such as Chōmei's *Hōjōki* (An Account of a Ten-foot-square Hut) and the *Heike Monogatari* (The Tale of Heike - an account of a battle between the Taira and the Minamoto) of unknown authorship recount the disasters of a *mappō* (decadent) society. At such times, man has neither the energy nor the interest to be involved in long philosophical discussions. Instead, he searches for a brighter outlook on life that can be obtained by the simplest and most direct methods. Shinran's claim that "if a virtuous man can gain enlightenment, then how much

easier must it be for the unvirtuous"[3] must have been reassuring for
the people of the time.

II. Establishment of the True Pure Land School

Many writers speak of Shinran as the founder of the True Pure Land
School. Although such a claim is in one sense acceptable, it is nonetheless an inaccurate statement. Shinran never considered himself a
founder of a Buddhist school and textual passages to the contrary are
impossible to find. We do know, however, by the way in which he signed his works, that Shinran considered himself a person of mediocre
talents. He signed his works, "...written by a baldheaded simpleton".[4]

Inspite of his claim to be a "simpleton", his works show signs of
great scholarship. His opus magnum, the *Gen-jōdo-shinjitsu-kyō-gyō-
shō-mon-rui*, is a work of great scholarly merit which explicates, sys-
tematically, the True Pure Land teachings according to scripture (*kyō*),
practice (*gyō*), faith (*shin*), attainment (*shō*).

By the term "scriptures" is meant the three basic *sūtras* of the
True Pure Land School. The three are:
1. *The Larger Sukhāvatīvyūhasūtra*
2. *The Smaller Sukhāvatīvyūhasūtra*, and
3. *The Meditation Sūtra*.

"Practice" means the *Nembutsu*, which is not self-motivated but is called forth, so to speak, when one realizes his great indebtedness to all
sentient beings for one's existence. "Faith" means the actual recitation of the Buddha's name, which is a spontaneous act. "Attainment"
refers to a state of joy, sincerity, and the desire to listen to the
Buddha's teaching, all of which result when one realizes one's indebtedness in life.

The *Kyō-gyō-shin-shō* was not written by Shinran for the purpose
of accumulating merits nor was it written to gain worldly fame. It
was written simply to clarify Shinran's own religious commitment for
himself. Thus, inspite of the fact that Shinran's works are considered to be the basic texts of the True Pure Land School and, as a consequence, Shinran is considered to be the founder of the School, it was
not his intention to establish a unique form of Japanese Buddhism. He
writes, on the contrary, "I have no disciples of my own".[5]

One may then wonder how it is that a True Pure Land School has
been established. Gradually, as the *Nembutsu* practice became popular
among people throughout Japan, jealousy arose among the monks who

adhered closely to the tradition of upholding strict disciplinary rules. When their feeling of jealousy reached its peak, the monks plotted for a political maneuver to have both Honen and Shinran removed from the ancient capital of Kyoto. Shinran was abandoned to the Kanto district, an area north of the present day Tokyo. Contrary to the jealous monks' original intention, the abandonment gave Shinran a golden opportunity to explain the *Nembutsu* to many people living in outlying areas. As Shinran walked to his place of exile and expounded the *Nembutsu* to the people along the way, the numbers of people who began practicing the *Nembutsu* gradually grew. After serving his term in the Kanto area, he was given permission to return to Kyoto and died shortly thereafter.

His remains were enshrined in a columbarium, the Otani Hombyo. At first, the columbarium was maintained by the *Nembutsu* adherents living in the Kanto area and Shinran's children, Kakushinni, Kakue and Kakunyō, were elected to be caretakers. Kakunyō, however, considered changing the status of the columbarium to that of a temple. Due to her efforts, the Hombyo came to be known as the Honganji Temple. Shortly thereafter, support from the Kanto area weakened and the temple was in an economic crisis until Rennyo (8 generations later) organized the small, separated groups into the True Pure Land School organization. Thus it was Rennyo who actually organized a True Pure Land School.

Gradually the True Pure Land School gained economic and political powers, so much so that it became a threat to Oda Nobunaga (1536-1598) who "virtually obliterated the greatest scholarly and religious center of ancient Japan"[6] when he destroyed the Tendai temple on Mt. Hiei. In his campaign to destroy anything that got in his way, he managed to dissect the Honganji power by dividing it into two - the Higashi (East) Honganji and the Nishi (West) Honganji. It was not until the 10th year of Meiji (1878) that the Higashi Honganji took the name "Ōtani-ha" and the Nishi Honganji took the name "Honganji-ha".

III. Transference to Canada

It was the Nishi Honganji Honganji-ha that responded to the religious needs of the Japanese immigrants who landed on the coastal areas of British Columbia and travelled inland to Southern Alberta in the late 1800s.

The manner in which the True Pure Land School was transplanted
into Canadian soil resembled the manner in which Buddhism was transplanted into China and Japan. That is, perhaps with the exception
of the Nichiren School (founded in Japan by Nichiren - 1222-1282) and
its sub-schools, proselytizing was never a salient feature of Buddhism;
thus, just as Buddhism "came along", so to speak, with the trade that
flowed between India and China on the Silk Route during the first century before Christ and with the migration of the Koreans and the Chinese into Japan in the sixth century after Christ, the True Pure Land
School "came along" with the immigrants from Japan when they crossed
the ocean to settle in the coastal regions of British Columbia and in
Southern Alberta.

The early immigrants to Southern Alberta settled mainly in the
Raymond area. A few families settled in outlying areas such as Hardiville, Coalhurst, Fort Macleod, Calgary and Edmonton. Those who settled in the cities earned their livelihood through business; those who
settled in Hardiville and Coalhurst went to work in the coal mines and
for the Canadian Pacific Railway; and those who settled in Fort Macleod
and in Raymond gained their livelihood through farming. Those immigrants came to the new land with the intention of staying a few years,
making a sum of money, and then returning to their homeland. As it
turned out, many of them passed away before their dreams could be fulfilled, and among the other, there are still those who have yet to return even for a visit. Those people left Japan during the Meiji (1868-
1911) and Taishō (1912-1925) periods in Japanese history.

The Meiji period was "...a period of nearly two decades during
which the Japanese unabashedly pursued the fruits of Western "civilization and enlightenment" (bummei-kaika)".[7] It was a period of revolutionary changes. Compared to the former Tokugawa Period (1600-1867)
during which time the Samurais reigned supreme and Japan had closed its
doors to foreign influence for over two hundred years, the Meiji her-
alded in a period in which the old Tokugawa slogan, "Keep out the Bar-
barians" was replaced by the belief that anything Western was superior.
The West symbolized modernization and the move to modernization was so
strong that there were those who firmly believed that a person who had
not travelled to the West could not be considered to be human. In the
Meiji period, the Japanese even toyed with the idea of making English
their native language. The glory of modernization, however, was not
long lived, as the Japanese soon realized that their customs and mores

of antiquity were also of value. Gradually the society turned towards old Confucian ideas of morality and education. Thus, by the Taishō period, Japan had nestled down in a hybrid society of Western modernizing influences and old Japanese traditions.

The immigrants to Canada came from such a cultural milieu. They brought with them the culture and language of the time and were successful in maintaining them until very recent times.

Even in an isolated place like Raymond, the Japanese have managed to survive with a minimal amount of English. It comes as a great surprise that the *Issei* (first generation) would have managed to remain in Southern Alberta for the past 50 or 60 years without feeling the need to learn the English language.

That the majority of those immigrants were proponents of a formal Japanese tradition becomes evident when one examines the attitudes with which they brought up their children, the *Nisei* (second generation). It is obvious that, prior to World War II, the *Nisei* was governed by attitudes found in the latter Meiji and Taishō Japan. For instance, when the young people in Raymond wanted to organize dance parties in the church, a special meeting of the executives took place and a resolution forbidding the children from having a dance in the church was passed. The reason for such a resolution was that to hold a dance would not only be a disgrace to the Japanese people, but even worse, to allow the young people to embrace in public would be devastating to the Japanese nation. Things have taken a turn and it is the senior citizens who once frowned on such actions who organize the dances now.

IV. Changes in the Japanese Pure Land Buddhism

Those senior citizens who left Japan during the Meiji and Taishō periods in their youth were founders of the first Alberta Buddhist Church in Raymond. On July 1, 1929, the Japanese who were living in the area gathered together at the home of Mr. Kyojun Iwasa for a Obon (Memorial) service. Reverend G. Taga, a resident minister of the Honpa Buddhist Temple in Vancouver, was invited to conduct the service. Directed by Reverent Taga's wish to see a Buddhist organization and a Buddhist Church established in Raymond, the people discussed the possibility of fulfilling his wish. The establishment of the Raymond Buddhist Church was spearheaded by Messr. Kyojun Iwasa, Yoshio Hatanaka, Yoichi Hironaka, Tanesabura Kosaka, Eita Sonomura, Takejiro Koyata, Kisabura Sugimoto and Buhachi Nishimura - all of whom are now deceased.

Mssrs. Yoichi Hironaka and Yoshio Hatanaka were elected to nego-
tiage with the Church of the Latter Day Saint for the purchase of
their old building. Transaction for the purchase of property and
building was completed for a price of five thousand dollars. The people then made a request for a resident minister. In order to finance
their project, they instigated a hundred-year plan. Under that plan,
the members were to pledge monies which would be paid during a hundred year period. If the one who made the pledge was unable to pay
his share, then his son or daughter would be held responsible. In
this way, the people accumulated the required amount of money to purchase their temple and to welcome their first minister, the Reverend
Shinjo Nagatomi.

Reverend Shinjo Nagatomi and his wife arrived in Raymond on June
4, 1930 to be greeted by the depression which demanded that the minister and his congregation seek a means of survival. Reverend Nagatomi
remained in Raymond until 1933 and was replaced by Reverend Yutetsu
Kawamura.

Reverend Yutetsu Kawamura, together with his wife and one daughter, came to Raymond in 1934. He remained until January, 1940, when
he decided to return with his family to Japan. En route, when he
reached Vancouver, he was asked by the Acting Bishop, the Reverend
Aoki, to remain in British Columbia at the Maple Ridge Buddhist Mission, because the minister there had passed away. Reverend Kawamura
decided to remain until a replacement minister could be found, but
with the outbreak of the war, he and his family were evacuated back
to Raymond.

The war and evacuation meant two things:

1. The uprooting of the Japanese people from their
   accustomed mode of life, and

2. A growth in Buddhist activities in Southern
   Alberta.

As a whole, the Japanese enjoyed a sheltered life in a ghetto
which they nourished and protected. Prior to World War II, the Japanese lived a life not unlike their counterparts in Japan. They were
accustomed to living in close proximity to each other and to using
their native language as a means of communication. Most of their
daily business was transacted in Japanese and it was not unusual to
see a Japanese shop for Japanese commodities in a Japanese owned department store.

To ensure that the Japanese language would continue to be the medium for communication, they established Japanese Language Schools, usually operated by the local Buddhist Churches. The children would attend their regular English schools during the day, and then after school, they would proceed to Japanese schools. Many of the students gained such competency and proficiency in Japanese that they could compose *Waka* and *Haiku* in Japanese.

For the most part, the Japanese were engaged in businesses such as operating department stores, food services, flower shops and in industries such as fishing, farming, and lumber mills. Because these occupations were considered to be more suited to the White Caucasians, the Japanese were constantly felt as a threat.

The White Caucasians had nothing to worry about, because all of their worries came to a sudden end with the evacuation orders. Almost overnight, the Japanese were uprooted and transplanted to areas in interior of British Columbia and Southern Alberta.

Those who were interned in the interior British Columbia were treated as quasi-war prisoners. They were put into huge concentration camps where they carried out all of the affairs of running the camp, except for matters relating to the outside. They were, however, treated well, having adequate sleeping quarters and sufficient food. The people in those camps were able to continue educating their children in the manner to which they were accustomed prior to evacuation.

It was probably due to the fact that all of the evacuees expected to return to their familiar areas near the coast that they were able to withstand the period of internment. Many of them left with only the bare necessities of life. Many of them left behind family treasures in their homes or on their properties where they had carefully buried them.

Those who evacuated to Southern Alberta found themselves on farms as beet labourers. Just as much as evacuation meant a sudden change in the Japanese life style, so too evacuation meant a sudden change in the life style of the farmers who were to receive them. Only a few farms were equipped to accommodate the people. Some form of accommodations had to be quickly put together, and therefore, it was not uncommon to see portions of barns and chicken coops renovated to accommodate the large influx of Japanese evacuees.

The evacuees, who were accustomed to working on five or ten acre farms or on a floor of a department store, had a rude awakening when

they found themselves in hundreds of acres of sugar beets. The seem-
ingly endless rows of beets had to be thinned, weeded, and irrigated.
To the inexperienced worker that meant long hours of back breaking
labour. From early before sunrise until late after sunset, the evacuees worked in the fields with the dream that one day soon they would
be able to return to their accustomed ways.

Their dreams were not fulfilled however. Weary as the life of an
evacuee may have been, it functioned as a basis for assimilating the
Japanese people into a Canadian milieu. When the Japanese people were
free to move about again, some returned to their cherished areas only
to find that they would have to begin all over again. Their homes, properties, and treasures were no where to be seen. Their homes had been
confiscated and sold. Others took the evacuation as an opportunity to
explore other areas in Canada; thus, many travelled to the East. In
this way, the evacuation gave the Japanese an opportunity to move into
areas, both geographical and professional, which may not have been possible otherwise.

For the Buddhist movement in Southern Alberta, evacuation meant an
increase of Buddhist adherents and a growth in Buddhist activities.
The Buddhists gathered in areas such as Taber, Raymond, Picture Butte,
Coaldale, and Rosemary, and when the Japanese were allowed to live in
the city, Lethbridge became a center of Buddhist activities. Those
people put their efforts together in establishing churches in their
respective areas. Thus, by the time the war ended, new churches were
built in Coaldale, Taber, Picture Butte, Rosemary, and Lethbridge.
Those churches were unified under an umbrella organization called the
Alberta *Kyoku*. The *Kyoku*, or area of ministerial jurisdiction, was
established with the establishment of the Buddhist Churches of Canada.
The Buddhist Churches of Canada, as it did then, consists of four
kyokus - British Columbia, Alberta, Manitoba and the East. These divisions were necessary because only a small number of ministers were
available to serve the needs of the people. The Alberta *Kyoku* functioned as the official policy-making body for the Buddhists in Alberta.
It took care of meeting the finances required to support the ministers
and in consultation with the ministers, it established ministerial
schedules. It was the official body which had liaisons with the Buddhist Churches of Canada to which it sent delegates.

In principle, the Alberta *Kyoku* was a worthy organization, but in practice, it was a ballpark for those who vied for power and prestige. It comprised elected delegates from the Raymond, Coaldale, Picture Butte, Taber, Lethbridge and Rosemary Buddhist churches and delegates from a group of Buddhists in Calgary. A president was elected from among the delegates and he acted as the chairman and spokesman for the group. Because the *Kyoku* had no constitution to guide it in its policies, on many occasions, the chair took it upon itself to veto anything he did not favour personally. As a consequence, the position of the chairman was sought after by the delegate churches, because if one of their delegates gained the rank of chairman, then the Alberta *Kyoku* would operate in the manner that, that particular church wanted. As one can visualize, this meant that the Alberta *Kyoku* could function effectively provided that the chairman was an honourable man, but if he were not then the *Kyoku* would be inefficient. Such was the situation in Alberta when Reverend Leslie Kawamura announced his return to Canada after his studies in Japan.

In 1963 when the announcement of Reverend Leslie Kawamura's return to Canada was made, the Alberta *Kyoku* was approached by the Buddhist Churches of Canada to inquire whether they would accept him as their minister. If the Alberta *Kyoku* were unwilling to accept him, then the Vancouver Buddhist Church would take him. Discussion as to what the Alberta *Kyoku* should do took place, but the chairman exercised his powers and would not allow it to come to a vote. The delegates from the Raymond Buddhist Church then requested that they be allowed to welcome Reverend Leslie Kawamura to their church as their resident minister. The chairman's reply was that if Raymond felt that they could finance him on their own, they should contact Reverend Leslie Kawamura personally and arrange for his return to Raymond, because the Alberta *Kyoku* would have no part of such a transaction. The Raymond Buddhist Church then contacted Reverend Leslie Kawamura and arrangements were finalized for his return to the Raymond congregation. When the arrangements were finalized, the Raymond Church reported this to the Alberta *Kyoku* and requested that their share of financing the Alberta *Kyoku* minister be cut back. Their request was accepted by the *Kyoku* and in 1964, Reverend Leslie Kawamura took up residence in Raymond.

The following year, the Lethbridge Buddhist Church requested a resident minister of their own on the basis that the Raymond Buddhist

Church managed to obtain its resident minister. The reply from the
Nishi Honganji was that if the affairs of the Alberta *Kyoku* minister
(Reverend Yutetsu Kawamura) would not be jeopardized by such a move,
then a resident minister would be sent to Lethbridge. With this, the
Lethbridge church requested support from the Alberta *Kyoku*. When the
question arose of how, without the aid of Lethbridge and Raymond, the
Alberta *Kyoku* could maintain the *Kyoku* minister, delegates from Lethbridge claimed that there was no need to discuss such an issue, because
when the Raymond Buddhist Church made their request for a resident
minister, the *Kyoku* did not have to deal with such a problem. Finally,
after months of deliberation, the issue came to a close with a disso-
lution of the Alberta *Kyoku*. At a meeting held on the evening of March
8, 1964, Reverend Yutetsu Kawamura resigned from his position as minister of the Alberta *Kyoku*. Delegates from the Lethbridge, Taber and
Picture Butte Buddhist Churches left the meeting, claiming that the
only official function of the chairman was to disperse the funds which
the *Kyoku* had. The other delegates who remained, wanted to work out a
solution which would enable them to have the continued services of the
ministers and so would enable them to continue their liaison with the
Buddhist Churches of Canada. The issue was pressing as a meeting of
the Buddhist Churches of Canada was scheduled to be held in Raymond on
the following day. They explained what had transpired on the previous
evening. A resolution was then passed to the effect that the organization which developed as a result of the efforts of the steering committee would be the official Alberta representation to the Buddhist
Churches of Canada in the future.

The steering committee which consisted of six elected people and
the two ministers met on many occasions in the days that followed.
Finally they drafted a constitution outlining the function and purpose
of the organization which they proposed to call the Honpa Buddhist
Church of Alberta. The term "Honpa" was essential as they wished to
keep their identity with their mother temple, the Honganji-ha Nishi
Honganji, in Kyoto. A detailed constitution in accordance with the
Societies Act of Alberta was necessary as they did not wish to repeat
the errors in organization policy that the old *Kyoku* displayed. Under
the constitution, the functions and the rights of each member and the
elected Board of Directors were clearly outlined. The Honpa Buddhist
Church of Alberta was to take charge of all affairs concerning the
ministers. No minister would be a resident minister of any member

church, but he would be a minister of the Honpa Buddhist Church of Alberta and serve the member churches in that capacity. Schedule of ministerial activities would be compiled in such a way that each member church would have an equal share of the minister's time. Membership in the organization was open to any individual, if he or she did not belong to a member church. A budget for a year's operation would be established and the members assessed accordingly. As a consequence of careful planning, the Honpa Buddhist Church of Alberta had an annual operating budget equal to the annual budget for the Buddhist Churches of Canada.

The establishment of the Honpa Buddhist Church of Alberta was not without hardships. While the steering committee was very busy planning the organizational structure and the constitution for the organization, the Buddhist Churches of Canada, under the pressure of those Buddhists in Alberta who were not in favour of the new organization, passed a resolution to the effect that those who did not favour the new organization would be the people with which it would have continued liaison. It was later disclosed that the change in the Buddhist Churches of Canada policy was due to the fact that, whereas those Buddhist who were in favour of the new organization would have the services of the ministers, those who did not favour it would not.

The founding members of the Honpa Buddhist Church were the Raymond Buddhist Church, the Rosemary Buddhist Church, the Coaldale Buddhist Church, and people who lived in Lethbridge, Picture Butte and Taber. People who lived in the last three districts were asked to leave their respective churches if they were going to support the new organization. As a consequence, those people congregated in schools, halls or homes to continue their religious services. Although the members of the Coaldale Buddhist Church unanimously passed a resolution to join the new organization, as time went on, the members, who opposed the resolution and who were discontented, proposed that the Coaldale Buddhist Church should leave the Honpa Buddhist Church of Alberta, because it did not have official recognition by the Buddhist Churches of Canada. This meant that in the event that a replacement minister was needed, they would be unable to obtain one. A vote was taken and although the poll was in favor of those who presented the new resolution, shortly thereafter, the majority of the Coaldale congregation left the Coaldale Buddhist Church to join individual members

in Lethbridge, Taber and Picture Butte. Together they purchased land
and within a few years built the Lethbridge Branch, Honpa Buddhist
Church of Alberta.

With the formation of a new church in Lethbridge and with the support of the Raymond and Rosemary Buddhist Churches, the Honpa Buddhist
Church of Alberta was now in a position to make plans for the future.
One of the issues that it had to confront was the creation of ministers. Because aid from either the mother temple in Kyoto or the Buddhist Churches of Canada was not forthcoming, the Honpa Buddhist Church
of Alberta established a scholarship fund to educate anyone interested
in becoming a minister. Unlike the old Alberta *Kyoku*, the Honpa Buddhist Church of Alberta was aware that unless Buddhism could be discussed in the English language, it would become a dead issue in Canada
and in Alberta. So long as the *Issei* (first generation) congregation
remains, there would be a need for a Japanese speaking minister, but
when the future is considered, the only medium which would be understood by a Caucasian or a *Nisei* and *Sansei* (third generation) congregation would be English. Thus, in the view of the Honpa Church, the
destiny of Buddhism in Alberta lies in the creation of English speaking ministers.

At the present time the Honpa Buddhist Church is working towards
that end. It grants a scholarship to Mr. Fred Ulrich, who is presently occupied as a teacher in an Edmonton public school, so that he can
study each summer at the Institute of Buddhist Studies in Berkeley,
California. Upon the completion of his studies, if he should so wish,
the Board of Directors will make provisions for Mr. Ulrich to work as
a full time minister of the church. If Mr. Ulrich decides not to work
as a minister, he is under no obligation to return the money.

While on the one hand, the church is planning for the future, it
has, on the other hand, taken positive steps toward actualizing its
future plans. Its acceptance of a Caucasian minister to administer
to the needs of the congregation - a first in the whole history of
Buddhism in Canada - is a landmark in Canadian Buddhism. The first
Caucasian minister to serve the Honpa Buddhist Church of Alberta was
Reverend James Burkey who administered to the needs of the people for
two years and then left for a teaching position in a small town just
north of Edmonton. The second minister to join, and who contributes
yet another landmark, is Reverend June King. She is the first woman
to serve any of the Buddhist organizations in Canada. She comes from

Fresno, California and is a mother of two children. She and her husband, Hue, work diligently for the furtherance of the True Pure Land teachings.

In the past, a priest was paid only a meager salary. He was expected to supplement his meager income with the *dāna* (charity) given by the members when they requested special family services. The Board of Directors of the Honpa Buddhist Church of Alberta who consider the priesthood as a professional occupation have budgeted for a minister's salary accordingly. Whereas under the old *Kyoku* system, a minister was expected to purchase his own car and pay for the upkeep of it, under the Honpa Buddhist Church system, all of the minister's expenses are met. Consequently, the church has established a policy that its members need not continue the act of charity for special family services. If, however, a member wishes to do an act of charity, he is not forbidden to do so.

The finances of the Honpa Buddhist Church of Alberta is met by assessing each member church according to its membership. Anyone who is 16 years old or older and who is self-sustaining is considered to be capable of paying assessments. Members over 65 are exempt. The church has special projects to augment its income. Special funds, other than operation costs, are budgeted so that the church can contribute to the development of Buddhism. The individual member churches are expected to meet the cost of maintaining the operation of their churches. In the event that a member church is in need of financial help, the Board of Directors request the other member churches to contribute funds.

The minister is in charge of all religious matters. He arranges for the regular Sunday services and the special services held throughout the year. Although the Sabbath has no religious significance for the Buddhists, it has been selected as the day for service because in a Christian oriented culture it seems to be the most appropriate day.

If one were to visit a Buddhist temple on a Sunday morning and observe the service which takes place there, one would conclude that it resembles any service one might observe in a Christian church. However, close examination would disclose certain differences. A typical Sunday service begins with a period of meditation. Unlike Zen Buddhism, meditation in the True Pure Land School does not involve sitting on mats in an erect posture. In the True Pure Land School, meditation is a period of silent contemplation during which a passage from

scripture is read. After the period of meditation, the congregation
joins the minister in what is known as *sūtra* chanting. The *sūtra* is
a class of Buddhist scriptures which contain the sermons delivered by
the historical Shakyamuni Buddha. The *sūtra* is chanted in English by
those who read in English and in Japanese by those who read in Japanese. After the chant, Sunday School students, who have been selected
to offer the incense, come forth to offer incense. The act of offering
incense is a symbol of pure intentions. During the offering of incense, the congregation sings a *gātha*. The priest then leads the congregation in scripture reading and following that he delivers his sermon. Another *gātha* is sung and the children are dismissed to their
respective class rooms. The minister and the Japanese speaking congregation remain in the chapel for a Japanese sermon and concluding
reading of scripture in Japanese.

In their classrooms, the children study the history and philosophy of Buddhism. They are taught patterns of behaviour which in the
days of the older *Issei* reflected Confucian moral standards but which
in the present day reflect the importance of understanding human in-
teractions in accordance with the Buddhist principle of causation.

Aside from the regular Sunday Services, special services are held
throughout the year. They are as follows:

1. Shu-sho-e   - New Year's Service held on January 1st.
2. Nehan-e   - Nirvana Day Service held in February.
3. Higan-e   - Equinox Service held twice yearly at
                    the times of the spring and autumn
                    equinox.
4. Hanamatsuri   - Buddha's Birthday Service held in April.
5. Fubo-no-hi   - Parent's Day Service: to express gra-
                    titude to one's parents; held in May.
6. Gotan-e   - Shinran's Birthday Service held in May.
7. Church Picnic - Held on picnic site in July or August.
   Service
8. Obon-e   - Memorial Day Service: to express one's
                    gratitude for the indebtedness to all
                    those who have passed away and who have
                    made Buddha's teachings available to
                    those who remain; held in July or in
                    August.

    9. Ho-on-ko   - Memorial Day Service for Shinran; held
                           in December.

  10. Joya-e   - New Year's Eve Service held at midnight
                           on New Year's Eve. The Church gong is
                           struck 108 times symbolizing the 108
                           emotions which man possesses.

Prior to World War II, it was also customary to observe the Emperor's birthday. Special services are held in commemoration of the 10th, 15th, 20th, 25th, 50th, and 100th year anniversaries of a church. On those occasions, special guest ministers are invited.

In contrast to the role that the True Pure Land School has played in Hawaii where all Buddhist religious days are civic holidays, the influence that the Buddhist church has exerted in Southern Alberta is infinitesimal, but not without results. The O-bon service, which served as the seed for the development of Buddhism in Southern Alberta, has had such an influence on the citizens of Raymond that the Town of Raymond has now officially declared the O-bon Service Day as the town's Memorial Day. As insignificant as this may seem, it is one instance where the West has made concession to the East.

The Japanese Folk Dance which takes place on the eve of the Lethbridge Branch O-bon service is much more subtle in its influence. On the eve of their O-bon service, the ladies from all the member churches gather in the Nikka Yūkō Centennial Garden to perform traditional Japanese Folk Dances. The ladies wear a Japanese attire called the *yukata* and perform the dances in a Garden designed in accordance with the Buddhist concept of the cosmos. Thus the dance in the Japanese Garden results in a complementary blend of Japanese culture and Buddhism.

V. Hypotheses Concerning the Future

1. To the extent that it is not out of necessity that a Japanese be a Buddhist or vice-versa, compared to other ethnic groups whose ethnicity is clearly defined by their religious beliefs, the relationship between being a Japanese and being a Buddhist is really one of confidence.

2. Were we to apply the usual measurements of ethnicity--race, language, food, dress, etc.,--to the Japanese, we would find that as the younger generations come to the fore, such standards for ethnicity would no longer hold. The reasons for that are twofold: (a) *assimilation* (b) *absorption*.

(a) *Assimilation:* The Japanese people are
gradually losing their ties with their homeland. As
the younger generations come to the fore, the Japanese eating habits, language and values will be replaced, if it has not happened to a large extent
already, by those more common in the Canadian scene.
The younger generations will be aware of themselves
as Canadians first and only secondarily, as of
Japanese ancestry.

(b) *Absorption:* More and more intermarriages
are taking place.[8] This means that the children of
those marriages will neither be Japanese nor Non-
Japanese. When those children marry, their children
will be less Japanese, and probably, more Non-Japanese.
A time will come when their ancestral background will
be neither important nor an issue.

3. The standards for determining ethnicity will have to be re-
examined and replaced by standards more akin to determining citizenship. That is, through assimilation and absorption, the younger generations of Japanese ancestry will gain behaviour patterns, eating
habits, and a sense of values which will mark them as Canadians.

4. In so far as Buddhism does not depend on a certain race for
its survival, even if, by absorption, the Japanese should become ex-
tinct, Buddhism would still survive, provided that some one person
continues to live as a Buddhist. This means that, in spite of the
fact that organized religious bodies have their functions, an organized Buddhist church is not an absolute necessity for the continu-
ance of the religion.

5. The assimilation of current Buddhist practices to those more
conducive to a Canadian ethnic group will not be detrimental to Buddhism, because Buddhism is "person" oriented rather than ethnically
or racially oriented.

6. The assimilation of Buddhist doctrines by disciplines such as
the sciences and arts will not threaten a Buddhist *weltanschauung*, because Buddhist doctrines are not "revealed" doctrines and because they
are principles which evolve from an examination of the human situation.

7. There is nothing in Buddhism which says that it must continue
at any cost. For a Buddhist, the continuation of Buddhism in any culture would be due to conditions favourable for its continuation and
its extinction would be due to conditions favourable for its extinction.

FOOTNOTES

1 The phrase, "the Buddhist way of Mt. Hiei", reflects a particular
   phase of Buddhist development in Japan. When Buddhism was first
   introduced into Japan prior to the Nara Period (710-784), it quickly gained the status as the source of learning. Thus, during the
   Nara Period, Buddhist temples served as places of learning where
   one could gain culture and education. However, with the move of
   the Capital to Heian (Kyoto), Buddhist temples played a different
   role. In the Heian Period (784-1185) Buddhist temples served as
   monasteries where the priests could practice various meditations.
   Thus, unlike the Nara period when temples were built right in the
   midst of a village or city, in the Heian period, temples were built
   high on the top of mountains. Characteristic of these temples were
   the Tendai temples on Mt. Hiei near Kyoto and the Singon temples on
   Mt. Koya in Osaka perfecture.

2 *Mahāyāna-sūtra-saṁgraha*, Part I, Ed. by P. L. Vaidya (Darbhanga,
   The Mithila Institute, 1961), p. 119, *Āryapratītyasamutpado nāma
   Mahāyanasutram:*

   > *Ye dharmā hetu-prabhavā hetuṁ teṣāṁ*
   >
   > *tathāgato hy avadat /*
   >
   > *Teṣāṁ ca yo nirodha evaṁ vādī mahāśramaṇaḥ //*

3 See, *Tannishō* in *Shinshū Shōgyō Zenshō* (*SSZ*; Comprehensive Texts of
   Shinshu, 5 Volumes; Kyoto, Kōkyō Shoin, 1940) Vol. II, p. 775.

4 See *Gen Jōdo Shinjitsu Kyō-gyō-shō Monrui*, in *SSZ*, Vol. II, p. 2.

5 See, *Tannishō*, in *SSZ*, Vol. II, p. 776.

6 Varley, Paul H., *Japanese Culture A Short History* (New York, Washington, Praeger Publishers, 1973), p. 97.

7 *Ibid.*, p. 163.

8 See, for example, G. Hirabayashi's paper in this volume.

JAPANESE HERITAGE, CANADIAN EXPERIENCE

When my father returned to Japan in 1952 for his first visit, it
was 45 years after his arrival in North America at the age of 19. He
had returned to Japan thinking of himself as a 100 percent culturally-
intact Japanese. After all, he had been living with a Japanese family,
participating in Japanese clubs, associations and churches, visiting
with Japanese friends, shopping at Japanese stores, eating Japanese
food, speaking Japanese. It didn't take him long to realize he wasn't
really a culturally-intact Japanese.

In the first place he had to straighten out his language. It took
him about a week to smooth that out--substituting certain North American innovations to real Japanese, words like Hawusu, tsurakku, bokkusu,
appuru, provinsu. And then he had to update some turn-of-the-century
words like *katsudo-shashin* (talking picture) to *eiga* (cinema). But his
greatest realization of gap was his point of view, the personal and
social orientation to life, and values. And on this, he found himself
unable and unwilling to resolve his differences.

My father returned after a five month visit very appreciative but
with a discovery that Seattle was his real home now. To put it briefly
and symbolically, he said: "When I die, I want to be buried here."
This was in sharp contrast to an earlier, vague notion that somehow he
ought to be buried in his home village in Nagano Ken when he died.

Four years ago, en route to a research project in Sri Lanka, I had
my first real visit to my father's village and with my Japan-side relatives. The visit was filled with anxiety for both my relatives and
for me because the familiar well-known names on both sides were now
gone; we were first cousins, but total strangers. The cousin who was
delegated to meet me at the railroad station in Matsumoto had another
concern: What could he do when he met me if this North American didn't
speak anything but English? I can still see his relief when I asked as
we approached each other hesitantly: "Shimizu-san desu ka?"

In my week's visit at the foot of the Japan Alps I not only became
pleasantly acquainted with my cousins and nephews and nieces, but I had
the opportunity of walking along the few remaining paths that existed
when my father was young, of noting the place where his old school used
to be and of experiencing a few other things of this nature. A strange

feeling came over me--I was discovering something of my own past, a part of me that I hadn't known. It was a good feeling, an enriching feeling.

When my father returned to Japan, he was shocked to discover a gap. When I visited Japan, I was pleased to discover a bridge. These contrasting experiences raise fundamental questions of our Japanese heritage--What is it? How much of the Canadian experience is rooted in Japanese heritage? And this is tantamount to asking, culturally, what of our Buddhist heritage is expressed in a Canadian perspective?

In discussing these questions, I propose to cover the following topics: 1 our Japanese heritage; 2 the Japanese pioneers as modifiers; 3 Japanese heritage Canadianized; 4 Japanese Canadian Identity.

1. Our Japanese Heritage

In his paper, "The Study of Japanese Personality and Behavior,"[1] William Caudill extracts from several sources the following common themes relating to Japanese character:

1. "A sense of the group or communality as being of central importance." This is a powerful emphasis that underlines the essential priority of the group, frowning on individualism.

2. "A strong sense of obligation and gratitude." This is another dimension of the emphasis upon the group, strengthening the bonds of group solidarity; the concepts *giri* and *on* (both referring to obligation) are central to the Japanese character.

3. "A sense of sympathy and compassion (*ninjo*) for others."

Typically, those three aspects of the Japanese personality express themselves in social functions with a symbolic gift of a quality appropriate to the social relationship and the occasion when calling upon a friend, or to rally as a community when aiding a friend rebuild his house in the case of a fire, or to interrupt work and other normal functions on the occasion of a death, and to a slightly lesser extent, a marriage.

4. "A strong sense of 'we' versus 'they'." Just as a group emphasis produces a strong in-group feeling of "we", so also there is a group focus towards others as "they". Under these conditions there is minimal attention to individual outsiders except as members of a "they".

5. "An underlying emotionality and excitability which is controlled by a somewhat compulsive attention to details, plans, rules." To the more informal Western eyes, this aspect appears to be the basis for an emphasis on form and protocol. At the turn of the century, an

internationally respected philosopher, Inazo Nitobe, observed, "Personally, I believe it was our very excitability and sensitiveness which
made it a necessity to recognize and enforce constant self-repression."[2]
Later, in the 1940s, a linguist and Buddhist scholar, Hajime Nakamura,
noted that "...the thinking of most Japanese tends to be intuitive and
emotional."[3]

6. "A willingness to work and to persevere toward long-range
goals." Here is an argument that the work emphasis, so strongly and
exclusively associated with the protestant ethic in the west, may well
have other sources for its expression.

7. "Devotion to parents, and an especially strong and long-endur-
ing tie to the mother persisting in almost its childhood form." This
deeply entrenched feeling of filial piety ties in closely with the respect for authority in an hierarchical social structure. Anthropolo-
gist Chie Nakano states that the Japanese society is vertically struc-
tured (*tatē*)[4] and an essential feature of such a society is respect for
authority figures, which in the family context would be filial piety.

8. "An emphasis on self-effacement and a tendency to avoid taking
responsibility for the actions of oneself or others." In a *tatē* society with strong emphasis on the group and with associated feelings of
giri and *ninjo*, a highly desired (for them) quality emerges which in
Japanese is expressed as *otonashii* (to be reserved and unassuming) and
enryo (a cluster of behavioral traits characterized as deference).
Moreover, in the lower echelon of a *tatē* society, such as among the
peasantry from which much of our Japanese immigrants came, a customary
mode of adaptation would be fatalism, or powerlessness, and is characterized in Japanese actions as *shikata ga nai* (it can't be helped) and
gaman (to forebear, to endure or to put up with).[5] Thus, in a *tatē* society of *giri* and *ninjo*, *otonashii* and *enryo*, *shikata ga nai* and *gaman*
we have the natural foundation and motive for social conformity. A
most apt aphorism which reinforces this emphasis is *deru kugi wa uta-
reru* (the nail that sticks out is the one that gets hit).[6]

9. "A tendency toward understatement and an emphasis on non-ver-
bal communication." Edward Hall, in his recent book, *Beyond Culture*,[7]
describes the communication breakdown that occurs between high context
cultures and low context cultures. In a low context culture, like the
North Americans, the essence of the communication is embodied in the
words, and therefore, the message contains details of what is intended
to be communicated. In a high context culture, like the Japanese, the
essence of the communication is in the context, i.e., in the setting,

socially and culturally, and thus would represent a put-down if spell-
ed out in western fashion.

10. "A pleasure in the simple things of life," such as being in
beautiful surroundings (bringing to our vocabulary the concept, *shibui*,
simplicity as in the avoidance of unnecessary claptrap which often de-
tracts from the "essence of beauty"); playing with children; bathing
(the great social institution, now rapidly disappearing in urban Japan,
of the community *furo* or bath, as similar to a swimming pool, but extremely hot, to which one enters after a thorough washing, and then for
a quarter of an hour or so boils in heavenly content); and drinking
(the social function of the *sake*, a rice wine served quite warm, which
literally releases, or at least establishes the legitimate social setting for the release of, the restraints to form and politeness and
stoicism that have earlier been detailed).

As a springboard for the kind of character background to which
our Japanese immigrants to Canada were socialized, we have reviewed ten
qualities that give us a glimpse of our Japanese heritage.

2. The Japanese Pioneers as Modifiers

There were certain features of the Japanese immigrants to Canada
which differed somewhat from that of the European immigrants. The
early group, those in the latter 1800s until 1910 or so, were predominantly, almost exclusively, single and male.[8] They were, moreover
young, from the late teens through the twenties, and came largely from
rural peasant stock.

An aspect of the Japanese *tate* structure contributed another feature of the immigrant characteristic; first born sons, the *chonan*, assumed the obligation of the head of the household and inherited the
family home and whatever else the household possessed; thus, the immigrants were largely other than *chonans*. The *chonan* assisted other
males in the household to get established where possible, but it was,
also, up to the others to seek some other farm or fishing property or
jobs. Among the peasantry this was not an easy endeavor, so that there
were strong push-factors not only to find resources abroad for themselves, but to go to "America" and help establish the family fortunes.[9]

Compared to other new immigrants to British Columbia, the Japanese
immigrants were relatively well-educated, nearly all had at least elementary school, some the middle school, and a few even had high school
diplomas.[10]

In summary, then, the early Japanese immigrants were young single males, from rural peasant stock (farming and fishing background), majority with elementary school education, and other than first sons for the most part. They came as *dekasegi* with the intention of returning to Japan in a few years relatively rich. This aspiration shifted as gold was not to be found by the roadside. The few years stretched out; the 1908 immigration restrictions reduced movements between Japan and Canada, and therefore arrangements for brides, the so-called "picture bride" movement, developed.[11] Thus, the *dekasegi* became a genuine settler, and a permanent part of the Canadian scene; communities emerged in the lower mainland and on Vancouver Island; and the second generation began to arrive. But a question arises: Were the Japanese values and characteristics described earlier brought over intact to Canada?

3. Japanese Heritage Canadianized

It is one thing to summarize from documented sources what appears to be the essence of the Japanese character. Those characteristics brought to Canada were dependent upon the culture-carriers, the Issei, and in time, the Isseis shaped in Canada a pattern different from that which their relatives were shaping in Japan. The peasant, rural perspective to Japanese ethos, qualified by the youthful male viewpoint, tended to exploit selectively their Japanese heritage as they coped with settlement in Canada. The harsh pioneering life forced special emphasis upon the hard-work ethic (*gambatté yaré*); this was in accord with the North American value of the protestant ethic. Postponement of immediate gratification and consumption also accorded with the western notion of planning and saving.

Confronted with legal restrictions (denial of citizenship and access to certain types of work) and general racism,[12] for the new immigrants, the sense of group and "we" versus "they" sustained a necessary defensive posture of social protection, ethnic self-help organizations, as well as the general social needs. But their tendency toward self-effacement tended to be misunderstood in the face of low context cultural interpretation; if the Issei thought so little of themselves, the dominant society had concluded that this group was unworthy of respect. In other instances, misunderstanding produced stereotypes such as, sly, inscrutible, untrustworthy, suspicious, or as La Violette put it, the two major anti-Japanese arguments were "threat against the standard of living," and "inassimilibility."[13]

The fact that they came from a low station of life in Japan made more acceptable one's place of disadvantage, in fact, to some extent with a measure of fatalism. The Japanese traits, in other words, facilitated knowing one's place, doing what is expected, and having the perseverance to do it.

4. The Japanese Canadian Identity

If the Issei accepted their lot with some sense of resignation, there were crisis periods where "enough was enough" and the *gambatté yaré* spirit came to the fore, as in the riot of 1907.[14] But in the long term perspective the Issei goals, for the greater part, were sublimated to that of their children. As one concrete measure of this, they supported education for the Nisei on "faith" far beyond any reasonable expectation of "pay-off" and at considerable sacrifice to their own immediate pleasures. Even though pre-war British Columbia gave little opportunity for higher level occupations, the potentiality for achievement was persistently established.

The Niseis (second generation) were intentionally exposed by the Issei to the central importance of the group and community. However, unlike their cousins in Japan, there was for a Nisei little reinforcement of this theme by the other social institutions; in Japan, the schools, neighborhood, business world, the entire ethos would support this theme. Instead, a Nisei was exposed to opposing themes at school, like "The squeaky wheel is the one that gets the grease." Note the emphasis on individualism, the opposite of the social conformism characterized in "The nail that sticks out is the one that gets hit." Through these conflicting and confusing exposures, the Nisei developed an adaptation mode of the quiet Canadian, akin to the theme in Hosokawa, *Nisei: The Quiet American*.[15] Here is the development of a personality pathetically eager to join the mainstream; the Nisei picked up at home a social conformism, but not all of the *gambatté yaré* spirit of resistance when "enough was enough." They have shunned Japanese language and culture in favor of the Anglo emphasis in Canadian life. They were, in some instances, "out-whiting the whites."[16]

A great part of the Nisei problem was the concentration of the Japanese in lower mainland British Columbia, and the existence there of specially restrictive legal, social and economic patterns. Also, at the time of World War II, the average age of the Nisei was in the upper teens, under 20 years. Therefore, it may not be totally unexpected under these circumstances, plus the conflicting social climate under

which they lived, that strong, concerted protest to the wholesale evacuation of all persons of Japanese ancestry did not materialize among
them. But this group internalized from both sides, Canadian and Japanese, the work ethic of material success. Consequently, in the wake
of broader social and economic horizons after the great war, the Nisei
became firmly established as a member of the successful middle class.

This is the foundation of the Sansei (third generation), now well
into the adult age.[17] This group, unlike the Nisei, grew-up within
the confines of a comfortable urban, middle class, English-speaking
and western cultural environment and values. Two distinct modes of
adaptation are visible: (1) Integrative assimilation mode, and
(2) Pluralistic mode.

Superficially, the two modes appear to be similar. They both
spring from not only comfortable middle class homes, but have grown up
in a Canada vastly different from the restrictive, pre-war days of the
Nisei youth.

(1) Integrative Assimilation Mode

Japanese youth, whether in Vancouver, Toronto or Lethbridge, no
longer live within ethnic enclaves. Moreover, while the pre-war Japanese Canadians were largely concentrated occupationally in farming,
logging, fishing, grocery, small hotels, and were restricted legally
from certain professions,[18] now they are in every imaginable field,
especially in the professional field, with only the exceptions of the
top management posts and in elective political positions.

Even with their Japanese face, the Sansei are blending into the
Canadian scene. So much so that in several cities in the United States,
intermarriage rates rose to "a startling 49 percent."[19] As recently as
1959, it was only 23 percent, and in 1948 it was but 12 percent. Similar reports have been published regarding other California cities.[20]
In the days when racism was more overt, and in many dimensions legal,
one way to put-down any argument in this sphere was "Would you have
your daughter marry a Japanese?" From this perspective and from the
findings in the United States, intermarriage rates appear to be good
indices of assimilation of the Japanese in the United States. What
about in Canada?

This writer had the opportunity in 1975 to investigate the marriage register of Taber and Lethbridge from the 1940s to the end of
1974.[21]

TABLE 1

INTERMARRIAGE RATES, JAPANESE CANADIANS

TABER, 1941-1974

Year	No. Total Marriages	No. Inter-marriages	Percent Intermarriage
1941-49	9	1	11.1
1950-54	6	0	0.0
1955-59	20	5	25.0
1960-64	11	2	18.2
1965-69	6	4	66.7
1970-74	14	10	71.4

Table 1 indicates some interesting rates. There was only one recorded intermarriage in the 1940s. The number increased to 5 in the
1950s, still just a sprinkling, and remains insignificant (just 2),
during the first half of the 1960s. But there is a spectacular rise in
the latter 1960s (4 out of 6), and for the first half of the 1970s it
increased to a high of 71.4 percent (10 out of 14). Was this a typical
rate for southern Alberta in general or was there some extenuating circumstances, such as, those who were intermarrying would be getting
licenses in Lethbridge (where there are more Japanese; and would also
be the logical place to register when one of the parties was from Taber
but the other was from Raymond or Picture Butte). What would the rates
at Lethbridge show?

From 1945 until 1970 there was a remarkable stability in the number of Japanese applying for a marriage license (from 71 to 77 for
5-year periods); it increases to 89 applications for the first half of
the 1970s. The Lethbridge intermarriage rates may best be described
as representing just a sprinkling prior to the 1960s. From 1960 to
1964 it rose to 31.9 percent, from 1965 to 1969 it broke past the fifty-
fifty ratio to 54.5 percent. For the first half of the 1970s the rate
was a phenomenal 82 percent. If the Japanese Americans are impressed
with rates that approach the 50 percent figure, what can be said for
Lethbridge?

With a rate of 82 percent both sexes are out-marrying. The record for the last full year recorded, 1974, showed that of the 22

TABLE 2

INTERMARRIAGE RATES, JAPANESE CANADIANS

LETHBRIDGE, 1942-1974

Year	No. Total Marriages	No. Inter-marriages	Percent Intermarriage
1942-44	32	0	0.0
1945-49	72	2	2.8
1950-54	73	4	5.5
1955-59	71	6	8.5
1960-64	73	23	31.9
1965-69	77	42	54.5
1970-74	89	73	82.0

licenses that were issued, 20 were intermarriages. Can there be some kind of deliberate ethnic self-rejection?

Not so, say the people in the area. This area, before evacuation, had only about 350 Japanese. Then came over 3,000 evacuees from the west coast in 1942, settling almost exclusively on sugar beet farms. Now, a third of a century later, the majority are in the towns of this area, in every conceivable occupation from mechanics, government service, engineers, teaching, "you name it, and I'll locate a Japanese in it."[22] One Nisei made the following observation: "When I leave my home in the morning, I have my work, lunch and recreation contacts with friends and fellow workers. But until I come home, and look at my wife, on many a day I don't see another Japanese face. If my experiences are like that, the Sansei must have similar ones. People usually marry those with whom they contact. No, the intermarriage rates are not all that surprising to me."[23]

An Issei woman spoke of her situation. "I have four children. My first two married other Nisei; my last two intermarried. At first I was very upset and disappointed. But now I am happy; my son-in-law is a school principal here and is so considerate and thoughtful of my daughter, and of me, too." A Nisei mother expressed only one major regret: "My children's choices are sacred and respected. I only regret, and this I feel very strongly, that they did not really have an

opportunity to choose between a Sansei or someone else. Sansei dating
somehow never occurred."[24]

The Southern Alberta intermarriage rates should not, without accompanying evidence, be generalized to the rest of Canada. But it is
this writer's hypothesis that the Japanese Canadian intermarriage rates
are well past the fifty percent figure; more specifically, the Vancouver rates may be around the 60 percent mark with Toronto, the largest Japanese Canadian population center, approaching the 70 percent
zone.

Under these circumstances it may not be unexpected to have the
"assimilationist Sansei" protest that he is not a Japanese-Canadian;
he is a Canadian, period. None of this hyphenated stuff. Among this
group, being a hyphenated Canadian represents a pejorative category,
something other than a "true Canadian." The Nisei, on the other hand,
are more inclined to view the hyphenated Japanese Canadian identity
with positive implications. When probed regarding the meaning of a
"non-hyphenated" Canadian and its characteristics, some of the Sansei
began to observe that what was initially regarded as non-hyphenated
turned out to be essentially a particular hyphenated variety, the
Anglo-Canadian.[25] This led to a re-examination by them of the concept
"hyphenated Canadian" and of whether all Canadians in some manner would
fall under that label and if so, of whether it should continue to be
held negatively.

(2) Pluralistic Mode

The other group, less in numbers, could be regarded as the "pluralistic" Sansei. They integrate structurally into the Canadian social
fabric, but with an effort to do so on the springboard of their Japanese heritage. They have already confronted the question of what a
Canadian identity involves, and have concluded that the most positive
direction to things Canadian would be to participate with *authenticity.*
city. In other words they challenge those who say "I'm not a Japanese
Canadian; I'm *Canadian*! My heritage is Shakespeare and Beethoven."[26]

The "pluralistic" group wonders why Shakespeare and Beethoven contribute to a Canadian heritage? In the first place, they represent a
cultural heritage applicable to many nationalities, and secondly,
neither have been to Canada (and Beethoven isn't even Anglo). The
statement "I'm not a Japanese-Canadian", implies that things Japanese
are not qualified to be imported as something Canadian and smacks an
inferiority complex which is overly compensated by such a statement.

The "pluralistic" Sansei feel it is much more healthy to enter the Canadian mainstream on the foundation of pride and respect as Japanese-
Canadians.

But here a dilemma arises. Their Nisei parents, for reasons mentioned earlier, neglected to give them a sound Japanese language and
culture foundation. There is a desire among this minority to fill the
gap, and they have sought language classes and cultural exposure (flower arrangement, odori, martial arts, along with history, literature,
philosophy, religion). Some of them have gained insights to their own
personality patterns (recognizing their own traits of reticence to
speak out in public, tendency toward self-effacement) which they hadn't
realized had ties with their Japanese heritage. They found out that it
was not just a personal thing.

The search for one's roots and the opportunity for youth groups of
similar inclinations to get together is much more facilitated among the
Buddhist group than among the Japanese Christians. The fact that language and culture are no longer prominent barriers toward a meaningful
religious service has made it possible for Christian Japanese-Canadians
to attend and to belong to community churches of their denominations.
Therefore among the Christian Japanese-Canadians, the youth groups are
integrated, ethnically. In contrast, the Buddhist members still find
that the youth are predominantly Japanese-Canadians, and that the situation presents an opportunity to explore new concerns of roots and
identity with others of similar bent. Also, the substance, style and
content of Buddhist beliefs and services are still fundamentally Japanese. The bridging to one's heritage is enhanced therefore.

In this paper I have explored the role of the Japanese (and by
implication, Buddhist) heritage to Japanese-Canadian current perspective. Selective and modification aspects were noted. What appears to
be emerging, and what current researches now underway in different
Japanese Canadian centers will need to verify, is a change in the current Japanese-Canadian posture. First there is the emancipation from
the posture of pathetic eagerness among some of the earlier Nisei to
enter the mainstream of Canada. Following from this a two-pronged Sansei perspective is developing:

(1) the wholesale integration in work, marriage, social activities toward the emergence of a Canadian identity (at most with merely a
reference from where their ancestors came and whose children, 4th generation, will be only half Japanese); and

(2)   those who are rediscovering the richness and value of being Japanese-Canadian as the route toward a meaninful Canadian identity, with the non-Japanese mate being frequently the more enthusiastic participant. (In this sense cultural heritage is not integrally tied to racial heritage; cultural heritage is more an aspect of ethnicity.)

FOOTNOTES

1 William Caudill, "The Study of Japanese Personality and Behavior," in Edward Norbeck and Susan Partman, *The Study of Japanese in the Behavioral Sciences*, Rice University Studies, Vol. 56, No. 4, Fall 1970, pp. 37, 52.

2 Inazo Nitobe, *Bushido: The Soul of Japan*, N. Y.: G. P. Putnam & Sons, 1905, pp. 109-110.

3 Hajime Nakamura, *Ways of Thinking of Eastern Peoples*, (rev. English translation) Honolulu: East-West Center Press, 1964, p. 531 (original book published in 1947).

4 Chie Nakano, *Japanese Society*, Berkeley: University of California Press, 1970.

5 James Hirabayashi, "Nisei, the Quiet American?", *Amerasia Journal*, Vol. 3, No. 1, 1975.

6 David Buchanan, *Japanese Proverbs and Sayings*, Norman: University of Oklahoma Press, 1965, p. 46.

7 Edward Hall, *Beyond Culture*, N. Y.: Anchor Press/Doubleday, 1976. A discussion of these issues also occurs in "How Cultures Collide," *Psychology Today*, July 1976.

8 Rigenda Sumida, *The Japanese in British Columbia*, unpublished M.A. thesis, The University of British Columbia, 1935, Chapter II.

9 At this period of immigration (early 1900s), the area from Vancouver to Los Angeles was simply referred to as "America." The home-village of Steveston, for example, the fishing community south of Vancouver's International Airport, is Mio-mura (the village of Mio) but it is popularly known even in Japan as "America Mura."

10 Sumida, *op. cit.*

11 "I wanted to return to Japan eventually. I would have returned if I'd made any money. But I couldn't make any money so I couldn't go back." U. Suzuki, in Daphne Marlatt, *Steveston Recollected*, Provincial Archives of British Columbia, 1975, p. 19.

12 Ken Adachi, *The Enemy That Never Was*, Toronto: McClelland and Stewart, 1976, Ch. One. This book is dedicated as follows: "To the Issei who prevailed."

13 Forrest La Violette, *The Canadian Japanese and World War II, A Sociological and Psychological Account*, Toronto: University of Toronto Press, 1948, pp. 5-8.

14 Adachi, *op. cit.*, p. 74 especially, but generally the entire third chapter. As well, the accounts in Marlatt, *op. cit.*, of the fishermen's strike, pp. 30-34.

15 Bill Hosokawa, *Nisei: The Quiet American*, New York: Wm. Morrow
    and Co., 1969.

16 *Newsweek* magazine, June 21, 1971, story on the American Nisei.

17 The manner in which an immigrant group arrived in Canada, largely
    within a 10 year age spread, sending for wives and starting a
    second generation approximately within a 10-15 year span, developed
    not only the usual generational differences, but a difference that
    is closely correlated with historical period. In terms of popula-
    tion distribution by age, therefore, there is a distinctive tri-
    modal tendency. Thus, there is more than the usual meaningfulness
    in reference to the Issei, Nisei and Sansei.
        Today, the Issei are largely gone, the surviving members are
    mostly in their 80s and 90s; the Nisei are in the 40-65 range, with
    the median around 50. The Sansei range between 10 and 40, with the
    median just beyond 20.
        Since World War II, largely from the mid-Fifties, there has
    been a small but a steady influx of new immigrants from Japan, the
    Shin Issei (literally, the "new first generation"). They are a
    group which will need to be included in future discussions of a
    Japanese-Canadian identity; some of this population category are
    moving into a second generation. But this paper is confined to the
    majority population of the pre-war immigrants and their subsequent
    generations.

18 Sumida, *op. cit.*, Ch. X. Restricted professions included pharmacy,
    education, and working on crown land. Doctors and dentists were
    eligible for licences, but in the early days the medical school
    would not admit Japanese students, and there was no dental school.

19 Harry Kitano, *Japanese Americans: The Evolution of a Subculture*,
    Englewood, N. J.: Prentice-Hall, 1976, 2nd Ed., and also discussed
    widely in the Japanese American and Japanese Canadian ethnic papers.

20 John Tinker, "Intermarriage and Ethnic Boundaries: Japanese Ameri-
    can Case," *Journal of Social Issues*, Vol. 29, No. 2, 1973.

21 Taber is a town in Southern Alberta's irrigation area with a popu-
    lation of about 6,000. Lethbridge is the metropolis of Southern
    Alberta with a population just under 50,000 and the seat of The
    University of Lethbridge.

22 From field notes, 1975.

23 Interview with Walter Koyanagi, co-publisher of *Taber Times*, a
    weekly newspaper (which in 1942 was most vociferous in objecting
    to the government plans of bringing the "enemy aliens" to that
    area).

24 From field notes, 1975.

25 A group interview with selected Sanseis in Toronto, May 1975.

26 "Don't Ape the Majority," G. Hirabayashi in the special New Years
    Edition of *The Pacific Citizen*, January 1, 1977, p. 1.

MUSLIMS IN CANADA: A PRELIMINARY STUDY

Several studies[1] have been written on Muslim immigrant communities
in Canada that attempt to explore the scope and progress of acculturation and/or assimilation of these groups into Canadian life and the
role of religion, if any, in aiding or impeding this process. These
studies offer valuable insights into the Lebanese communities in Alberta but do not deal with the complexity of responses to the Canadian society by educated, Westernized professional Muslims who emigrated to
this country from other parts of the Muslim world. Furthermore, these
studies do not deal with the role of ethnicity within the Islamic community itself.

This essay therefore will attempt to give an historical overview
of the establishment, growth and administration of the Islamic community in Canada, the pressures and conflicts the community experiences
in the Canadian environment and the means utilized to resolve these
challenges.

Historical Background

Muslim individuals began coming to Canada at the turn of the century. (The earliest Muslim I could document came in 1898.)[2] They were
mostly young men from farming communities with little formal education
who came to the new world in search of work. The majority of those who
came during this period were from Lebanon. (They had been preceded by
about ten years by Lebanese Christians.) However, there were some from
Syria, from Morocco, from Albania and from Turkey.

Few of these immigrants went into farming. The majority, hampered
by the lack of facility in either French or English, became pedlars or
worked in the sweat shops, factories, and the mines where language did
not impede their productivity. Upon accumulating capital some became
independent store keepers or opened small businesses. The original in-
tent of most of them was to accumulate as much money as they could in
the shortest time possible and return to their home countries. Most
lived frugally sending money back to relatives (in some cases wives and
children) in Lebanon and many did return and purchase land there. Their
success spurred others to follow suit. Those whose savings were tied up
in businesses that could not be liquidated without excessive loss found
in the repeated upheavals in the Middle East cause to postpone the day

of return. Others who were not successful persevered in Canada, unwilling to return as failures.

Initially, Muslim immigration to Canada was limited to a very
small number. When the policy of peopling Canada was liberalized to
accept substitutes for British Protestant Subjects whose number had
dwindled, a few more were allowed into the country to join their relatives. The Syrians were ranked second from the bottom[3] in priority
(followed by the Chinese), and were considered of "inferior stock" because of racial, linguistic and cultural differences from the British
Protestant Subject ideal.

After the First World War the number of Muslims coming to Canada
was very limited. Employment opportunities in Lebanon increased due to
the French occupation of that country and the recruitment of young men
into the army. Furthermore, the occupation made it easier for Lebanese
to travel to other parts of the French Empire, especially West Africa,
where several Lebanese trading colonies were established.

The number of immigrants to Canada began to increase after the
Second World War. The new immigrants came mainly from Lebanon and
Palestine.[4] The fifties brought more Muslims from Eastern Europe,
Egypt and Lebanon. Although some of these immigrants, like the earlier
group, hoped to return to their home countries, most came with their
families to settle and make Canada their permanent home. The Palestinians had lost their homeland, Eastern Europe was under communist rule,
Egypt had a socialist government that had nationalized industry and
confiscated the property of the wealthy, and Lebanon's Christians were
monopolizing economic and political power.

When the Canadian quota system was abolished, more Muslims came as
settlers. They were mostly college educated professionals (doctors,
engineers, lawyers and professors) and disillusioned intellectuals who
found no avenues of employment or freedom in their home countries.
This group of settlers came with the intention to stay in Canada and
participate in its economic prosperity and free democracy. They were
admitted on the merit system and as such not only had a mastery of the
language, but were also partially or totally Westernized and urbanized
before arriving in this country. Pre-dominantly of Indo-Pakistani background, this group also included Muslims from the Arab world and other
Muslim countries.

Between 1966 and 1970, another wave of Muslim immigrants arrived.
They were mostly semi-skilled workers of Indo-Pakistani background who
were fleeing discrimination in Great Britain and East Africa. Also

arriving at this time were immigrants from Egypt, Turkey, Lebanon, Palestine, South Africa, Trinidad, Fiji, Mauritius and Guyana.

Thus the Islamic community in Canada is composed of persons from varied national and linguistic backgrounds. While the majority are of Indo-Pakistani origin, they are divided into East Pakistani and West Pakistani or into Urdu, Bengali or other speaking groups. The second largest group comes from the Arab world, mainly from Lebanon, with a substantial group of Egyptians and Palestinians and others from Syria, Morocco etc.

It is estimated that there are at present about 100,000 Muslims in Canada,[5] of whom more than three fifth are foreign born. The majority are urban dwellers. Toronto has some 40,000 Muslims and Montreal about 15,000. (Only about two thousand of each of these two cities are of Arab background.) Those of Lebanese origin are concentrated in Edmonton (5,000), Calgary (4,000), Windsor (1,500), London (1,500) and Lac la Biche (42 families). There are some Lebanese in most other areas including those who settled in Regina and Saskatoon around 1910.[6]

Although the first community to build a mosque in Canada was Edmonton in 1938, it was not until the late fifties with the new influx of immigrants that other mosques and Islamic centers were organized. These are located in Calgary, Halifax, Hamilton, London, Montreal, Ottawa, Toronto, Vancouver and Windsor. Several Islamic societies were formed in the seventies including Millat, the Croatian Islamic Center and the Ontario Muslim Association in Toronto, the Fatima mosque in Montreal, the Muslim Society of Sudbury and Thunder Bay and the Winnipeg Mosque. There are several Muslim organizations that do not as yet own a mosque or center or have recently been organized. These include Brantford, Cambridge, Kingston, Regina, Saskatoon, Thunder Bay, Sudbury, Waterloo and Wellington.

A substantial number of the twenty-two centers and associations mentioned above cooperate with the Council of Muslim Communities in Canada.[7] The CMCC has been seeking national recognition to function as a liaison between Canadian Muslims and other groups on the national and international level. Initiated by delegates from the provinces of Quebec and Ontario in an April 1972 meeting in London, it absorbed the only Islamic regional community organization in existence at the time, the Ontario Council of Muslim Communities (established 1969).

It is also estimated[8] that there are 20,000 Ismaili Muslims in Canada, of whom 5,000 live in Metropolitan Toronto. They are of Indo-Pakistani origin and are highly organized into *Jamaat Khanas*. They are

affiliated with the CMCC. The Muslim community also includes several
other Shia groups[9] and two mosques[10] of the World Community of Islam
in the West (formerly Black Muslims.)

A splinter group composed mainly of North American converts and
centered around the personal leadership of Dr. Baig, a professor in the
Department of Islamic Studies at Toronto University, split from the
Jami Mosque in 1967 and has been operating since 1971 under the name of
the Muslim Society of Toronto concentrating on the study and practice
of esoteric Sufism.

Also active on Canadian campuses is the Muslim Student Association
of the United States and Canada (started in 1962) with headquarters in
Indianapolis, Indiana. Its aim is to provide Islamic nurture through
education and "community" for students of Muslim countries in the hope
that they will provide Islamic leadership for religious reform in their
home countries upon their return.[11] The association also attempts to
provide guidance for living the Islamic life in the materialistic North
American environment.

The CMCC is a member of the Federation of Islamic Associations in
the United States and Canada (numbering over 200 communities and associations) with headquarters in Oldbridge, New Jersey.[12] The FIAUSAC
has recently received support, and the promise of aid from the Muslim
World League[13] (Rabitat al-Alam al-Islami) with headquarters in Saudi
Arabia. The Secretary General of the Muslim World League visited some
Canadian Muslim communities this summer and promised financial assistance for the construction of mosques in several cities. Grants have
also been received by the CMCC from the General Secretariat of the Organization of the Islamic Conference[14] (also with headquarters in Saudi
Arabia), to help in its different educational and social programs, including the publication of the magazine *Islam Canada*.[15]

The challenge that faces Muslims in Canada is not only dependent
on what Canada is--whether it is a multicultural society, or one that
subtly promotes Anglo conformity or an uncertain aggregate of peoples
of all nations arrested in a stage of identity crisis; it is also conditioned by what Islam is and who the Muslims are.

Islam as a way of life was revealed by God in the *Qur'an* and was
implemented by the Prophet Muhammad in the society at Medina between
622-632 A.D. Thus the prototype of the perfect society was experienced
in history under divine guidance and prophetic leadership - an example
set for posterity. After the death of the Prophet, the struggle over
the legitimacy of the succession precipitated a division of the Ummah

between those who tolerated secularization in the administration to preserve the unity of Islam and those who strove for the legitimacy of an
Islamic order. The latter eventually won, thus providing a wealth of
material describing ideal Islam where there is no separation between
religion and state.

Throughout Islamic history few have dared to call into question
this ideal or to try to adjust it to the prevailing reality, in which
the Muslim community was ruled by those capable of usurping power
through military might, frequently reducing the legitimate religious
leader to a figure head or a mere puppet. The abolition of the Cali-
phate by the Turkish regime in the twentieth century did not diminish
the commitment to the ideal[16] nor did it provide a consensus of Muslim
opinion to adjust to existing reality.

While contemporary Islamic literature continues to advocate the
restitution and maintenance of the ideal of the unity of the religious
and the temporal, a large number of Muslims throughout the world continue to lead secularized lives. In fact, several Arab countries have
adopted an official policy of Westernization and secularization (although some continue to pay lip-service to the ideal.) Thus secularization is a problem Islam faced thirteen centuries ago and rejected in
favor of the ideal which continues to haunt Islamic society in the East
and the West.

The rise of Arab nationalism as a response to Ottoman rule and
Western colonialism culminated in raising a generation of Muslims all
over the Arab world whose primary identity is a national, i.e. Arab,
rather than a religious one. The case of Lebanon may be an exception,
given the religious division of that nation. The story is often told
of the American student who went to register at the American University
of Beirut. He was asked by the registrar, "What is your religion?"
The student replied, "I'm an atheist." The registrar then asked,
"Christian atheist, Muslim atheist, or Jewish atheist?" Meanwhile, a
great number of Muslims in Lebanon identify with Arab nationalism as
expounded by Nasser.[17]

Of course a case can be made that the term Arab is an ethnic identity. For many Syrians, Jordanians, Palestinians, Lebanese and Iraqis
(and maybe others), however, it is an identity to transcend the religious division of the community, a division that was abused by Western
nations from the sixteenth century on. It is also conceived as an identity to transcend the geographical divisions of nation-states that the
Arab world was divided into after the Second World War.

Meanwhile, the Muslim Brotherhood and other traditional Muslims have repeatedly objected to this primary identity as one that discriminates against other Muslims in favor of co-nationals. After the 1973 war with Israel, one can note a resurgence in emphasis on a primary identity as Muslim. This is advocated by Saudi Arabia which is able to wield power through its financial support of different Arab countries. It is also heightened by a view that sees the war as a victory for the Arabs and a vindication of Islam. The Qur'an is quoted as being explicit that victory will be given to those who follow the path. The "Crossing" of the Suez Canal is seen in "Exodus" dimensions as a fulfilment of that promise. Previous defeats are thus attributed to the failure of Muslims to adhere closely to the true faith and to their having placed trust in socialism or in armaments.

These conflicts in identity are accentuated in the Canadian environment due to the fact that Muslim immigration to the North American continent is very recent (the majority having come after the Second World War), and that it represents different racial and linguistic backgrounds. For the Indo-Pakistanis, the primary identity tends to be Islam (over against Hindu) which has been fostered through the British policy of discrimination in India. The right to establish an Islamic state where Muslims can be Muslims was won through war and bloodshed, but its implementation continues to be nebulous due to lack of consensus on how it can be achieved, and whether it is to be a model modern state or a replica of the ideal state in Medina.

Islam as a total way of life is also a culture that has developed over the centuries an intricate system of laws and customs by which the true Muslim is expected to abide. Besides the religious laws, legislation includes all areas of political, social, economic and personal life down to the minutest detail. The laws are seen by most as divinely revealed or inspired and are therefore valid for all Muslims at all times in all places. In its spread across the world Islam encountered many alien cultures, some of whose customs were initially borrowed only to be rejected as innovation later on. In fact, what Islam could not assimilate, it ascribed to the non-Godly.

Thus although the North American experience is recent for Islam it is not unique, nor is the struggle with the materialistic forces of the "West" limited to those who have emigrated to the new world. Islam as revealed in Mecca was a rejection of crass materialism and the advocacy of mutual cooperation and responsibility towards one another as an expression of gratitude and commitment to God.

Specific Areas of Stress and Conflict

Islamic commitment is to be expressed in praxis. Each Muslim is
to announce his intention to follow the path daily by repeating the
Shahadah (witness) that there is no God but God and that Muhammad is
His prophet, and performing the ritual prayer five times a day. He is
to pay the *Zakat* (tithe), to fast the month of Ramadan and to go on a
pilgrimage to Mecca at least once during his lifetime. Three of these
essential elements of the faith are threatened in the Canadian environment, which although not hostile to the practice of Islam, does not
attempt to facilitate it.[19]

There are no minarets to call the faithful to prayer, nor is time
provided for the performance of prayer during the working hours. Interviews with Muslims of different national identities showed that
those who had been faithful in performing this tenet of Islam in their
home country began to be slowly negligent in their fulfilment of this
duty. For one thing, the long Canadian working hours and television
tend to keep people up later in the evening, and since most Muslims
live in cities they tend to rise later than is customary in the Arab
world and Pakistan. The law, though insistent that these prayers be
performed at prescribed hours of the day, has provided alternate times
for performing them in cases where it is not appropriate to pray at the
appointed time. It appears that once the Muslim begins to compromise
on this, he tends to slack off and prayer is reduced to once or twice a
day.

The fast of the month of Ramadan extends from before dawn to after
sunset. Since the lunar calendar is used, the month may fall during
any part of the year. If it comes during the summer months the dura-
tion of abstention from any food and drink is very long. Canadian em-
ployers do not take into consideration the difficulties that Muslims
face during this month and do not make any allowances for it.[20]

The paying of the tithe on income and possessions to be used in
the cause of Islam and to help the poor is an integral part of Islam.
Some Muslims excuse their neglect of this practice by saying that it
would be double taxation, since the state takes care of the poor out
of tax money. Some Canadian Muslims appear to be perturbed by this.
When Muslim scholars from abroad visit Islamic communities in Canada,
the question concerning the possibility of accepting taxation in lieu
of tithe is invariably raised in the hope that some kind of legal opinion can be cited to alleviate this duty.

The practice of usury is banned by the *Qur'an*. Some Muslims question whether borrowing from the bank is to be seen as usury.[21] Like other North Americans, Muslims borrow money from the bank to start businesses, to buy houses and in at least three cases in Calgary, London and Windsor to build mosques.[22] Many also receive interest on saving accounts or shares they own. The tendency is to explain this deviation from ideal Islam through one or more of the following reasons: that it is increasingly becoming a common practice in the Arab world, that it is a necessity for making a living and one has to adjust to the realities of the new environment,[23] that interested received barely covers the rate of inflation thus not changing the net worth of the capital or by finally pointing to the fact that the interest is paid to a bank and not to an individual.[24]

Another concern is the Muslim ban on the eating of improperly slaughtered meat. The Pakistanis tend to be more conscious of this, a fact that could be ascribed to the conditions in the Indian sub-continent. The Arabs, on the other hand, tend to accept the legal opinion issued to Muslims in South Africa sanctioning the eating of meat slaughtered for Christians.

Another restraint connected to food is the ban on eating pork. Most Muslims whether they are practicing or not tend to take this injunction seriously. They are careful about the bread they buy and avoid all food that might contain lard. In 1975, The Muslim Student Association circulated a letter received from Kraft Cheese Company explaining that due to the shortage of enzymes from cows for use in processing cheese, a supplement is added from pig enzymes. Most Arab Muslims questioned had not heard of this. Muslims of Pakistani background who were aware of the fact explained their consumption of cheese by reporting that the enzyme was a chemical agent and did not therefore become an integral part of the cheese.[26]

Sexual freedom in Canadian society is a source of stress for committed Muslims, especially bachelors. Since Islam considers any sex act out of wedlock as adultery to be punished by stoning to death, even the shaking of hands with a woman would necessitate the performance of ablutions for a conservative Muslim.

Other areas that infringe on Muslim practice deal with the personal status laws. Islamic inheritance law ascribes to females (mothers, wives and daughters) a different proportion than Canadian law requires. The writing of wills[27] specifying the Islamic shares is being advocated

among Muslims as the fulfilment of God's will and the preservation of
Islamic practice from the infringement of western interference.

In Islam, the man has the unquestioned right of divorce. Thus
Canadian law is seen to favor women, allowing wives to seek divorce and
to gain custody of the children.[29] This gives them the right to ali-
mony and child support.[30] Furthermore, whereas Islamic law provides
for speedy divorce procedures, some provincial laws (e.g. in Ontario)
specify a three year separation period.[31]

Islam gives women the right to property, to inheritance and to
keep their maiden names. Although they are seen as equal to men in
responsibility before God, their role is perceived as different from
that of men. The *Qur'an* gives the right of the administration of the
home to the man as he is the supporter of the family.[32] Several Muslims informed me that Canada is good for women; it gives them more than
their rights, especially Canadian civil law which forbids polygamy.[33]

Girls are restricted from dating, whereas boys tend to date Canadian girls. The restriction on girls is due to the fact that Islam
does not allow the women to marry outside the faith, whereas the men
can marry Christians and Jews. Furthermore, there is a double standard
towards children. Females are seen as something vulnerable that needs
protection. It is the man's right to attract women, but the virtuous
ones do not respond. The Indo-Pakistani community is generally younger
in age and has not faced this problem in a major way. Several suggested that they would consider returning to Pakistan in order to preserve
the honor of the girl. Some have talked about sedning their daughters
home to be educated or married, while others have already done so.[34]

The concern over the raising of children in the Canadian milieu is
not restricted to the conservative parents, rather it is shared by all
Muslims, especially those with daughters. Many are opposed to sex education in public schools,[35] while a few in Toronto have appealed to
have their daughters excused from participating in gym classes because
the required shorts are considered inappropriate attire. Others are
actively seeking the establishment of separate Islamic schools where
standard of dress, behavior and instruction can be guided by the Islamic
way of life. Efforts for such an endeavor are under way in at least
three cities - Edmonton, Montreal and Ottawa.

Concern about raising children in the Canadian "pornographic culture" appears in some of the Muslim writings in Canada. An unsigned
article says, "So what can we provide them with that will at least save
them from drowning into this world of pop art and pop music, groovy

clothes and groovier hair styles, smokes and snuffs that fly them high,
this world that is turning God's great gift, the desire for procrea-
tion, into a source of gay, free, swinging and unprincipled way of
life akin to animals."[36] This concern was voiced repeatedly by committed and secularized Muslims alike. Pornography is an evil threat
to the welfare of society as Islam advocates the disciplining of sexual instincts and desires and the chanelling of their fulfilment in
the marriage relationship. One father told me, "When we go for a walk,
I deliberately steer my children away from bookstores because I don't
want them to see pornographic material. This makes me feel bad as Islam encourages learning - but this, this is evil!"

All Muslims I interviewed agreed that it is easier to be a Muslim
in an Islamic country. For in Canada, the Muslim's commitment is tested daily and any justification he provides for deviation from the ideal
and participation in a secularized life takes him out of the domain of
Islam.

Is Islam in Canada an Ethnic Identity?

The answer has to be no. Islam as a religion transcends national
and geographical divisions. It is open to all mankind and is no way
restricted to any group. In its history Islam has had to deal with
peoples of different national and linguistic identities. Wherever it
spread, the ideal of one *Ummah* under God has been its motto. The policy of multiculturalism in Canada is welcomed by some Muslims because it
helps provide the financing for the teaching of Arabic; however it is
treated with suspicion because it helps breed division.

Islam has never sanctioned divisions, yet ethnic preferences within the community have surfaced in several ways. For example, at the *Īd*
celebration in Montreal, the Egyptians gathered in a separate room and
began an entertainment program using their own songs, folk dances and
dialect. Other Arabs joined the Indo-Pakistani Muslims in a more staid
celebration where there were recitations from the *Qur'an* and where the
program was in English. Furthermore, the Arabs tended to sit with their
wives while the Indo-Pakistani men sat in the front rows with wives and
children sitting in the rear.

Other ethnic preferences appear in the all-night retreats at the
mosques that seem to appeal to those of the Indo-Pakistani background.
One Pakistani leader told me, "We worship together but then the Pakistanis go back to their curries and the Arabs to their Kebabs." Thus
the mosque provides an affirmation of the universality of the Islamic

faith, but has not as yet provided for the social integration of the different national groups. Different ethnic allegiances tend to go to different mosques. This is true in Montreal where the Fatima mosque seems to attract a predominantly Arab congregation, while the Quebec Islamic Center appears to draw more Indo-Pakistanis. It is also true of the Ontario Muslim Association in Toronto which is predominantly Carribean and West Indian.[37] In other cities, it has been noted that after the Sunday service, groups tend to congregate according to ethnic identity.[38]

English, the leaders conceded, has become an Islamic language. Used as the vehicle of instruction and communication, it helps transcend ethnic insularity. Translations of the *Qur'an* into English by Yusuf Ali and Pickthall are distributed to all members, as are books on Islamic subjects published in Pakistan.[39] Meanwhile, although the sermon may be given in English, all quotations from the *Qur'an* and the *Sunna* are given in the original Arabic as well.

Most mosques attempt to operate a Sunday school where instruction in the Islamic way of life and Arabic language is provided.[40] These programs do not appear to be too popular among the young who complain that the instructional material is too boring and unattractive.[41] A survey of several mosques showed that the volunteer teachers felt that they needed additional training.

The congregational services in the mosque are usually held on Sunday. Although several mosques have Friday prayers, few members are able to attend. Because of this adjustment to the Canadian reality, the service has one sermon instead of the usual two.[42] The *Salat* (ritual prayer) on the other hand continues to be performed in Arabic.

Despite the fact that Islam has striven for uniformity and conformity throughout its history, Islam in Canada cannot at present be ascribed an ethnic identity because the Muslim communities vary in national and geographic origin, mother tongue, racial and physical characteristics, consciousness of their heritage, their values, their primary identity, their recent experiences as a peoplehood and their emotional attachment to their roots.

It must be remembered that the majority are first generation immigrants and are the objects of overt and covert discrimination and vilification by the rest of the Canadian society. Whether the hostility they encounter will weld them into an ethnic group is too early to predict. Meanwhile it is a factor that needs to be taken into

consideration, for many immigrants become aware of their "ethnic" identity only when it is ascribed to them by Canadian society.

Meanwhile, incidence of inter-marriage between Arabs, Indo-Pakistanis, Croatians, Turks and Carribeans is very rare. When it has occurred, the spouses encounter the usual problems of "inter-ethnic"
marriages. However, the leadership of the Islamic community is con-
fident that this is a passing phase and that Islam continues to provide
the mechanism for diversity and true multiculturalism.

A stereotypical image ascribed to the immigrants by the host culture through the educational system and fostered by the media may lead
to mutual distrust among Muslims. A study of seventy social science
textbooks used in Ontario schools (and other parts of the country)
showed that the adjectives "most frequently associated with Arabs included wild, uncivilized, nomadic, backward, disorganized and militant
against Israel."[43] Thus the Indo-Pakistani and Turkish Muslims may begin to identify the Arabs with the prototype perpetrated as wasteful
spendthrifts of the wealth that the oil provides, as the sole cause of
disruption of Western economies, as direct instigators of world inflation, as the cause of the perpetuation of poverty and hunger in the
third world etc...The Arabs, on the other hand, may feel that they have
enough prejudice to deal with without being associated with the Indo-
Pakistanis who are at present suffering from overt discrimination in
different parts of Canada.

The Role of the Mosque

It was mentioned above that early immigrants intended to return to
their home countries. Some studies refer to them as pioneers. This
appellation is appropriate only in the sense that they proved for those
who followed that immigration can be beneficial. However, seen from
the perspective of the Canadian society, this group of immigrants should
more appropriately be called migrants. Their frame of reference continued to be the home country. They did not think in terms of contrib-
uting to the host society, of participating in its future or of learning the majority language. For all practical purposes, they continued
to live their lives unaffected by their surroundings. It was their
children, tempered by the fire of marginality and anxious to gain respectability and acceptance that began to think in terms of identity
and of institutions. Supported by the new wave of immigrants whose intention was to settle in Canada, they began forming Islamic associations
and building mosques. While settlers hoped that mosques would provide

the institutions necessary for the perpetuation of the faith, those of the second generation had moved into the middle class society and sought to provide the social and religious institutions characteristic of that group.

Mosques have no exclusive religious significance. They have functioned in the history of Islam initially as a place of gathering to express commitment to the faith and the community and as a place of worship. They soon developed into centers of dissemination of political news and into educational institutions. In the Canadian environment, the mosque has acquired an added role. It has become a center of social and community activity, a place for the sharing of joy at weddings and of grief at funerals.[44] Women have become involved in the functioning of the mosque, attending the Sunday prayer,[45] teaching in Sunday School and assisting in fund-raising activities. Furthermore, the political function of the mosque has been lost as those of Indo-Pakistani origin oppose any political discussions such as the Israeli aggression in Palestine which is of primary concern for those of Arab background.

New mosques[46] that are erected reflect further environmental influences. They tend to have a meeting room adjacent to the worship area or a basement for use in social gatherings. (The new Calgary Mosque is the first to have an apartment for the Imam built next to the mosque.)

The organization of Muslim centers in Canada was initiated by the believers. (The Calgary association was formed in 1958. In 1960 they rented a mosque; each of the thirteen members paid the rent for one month.) Because the congregations were supporting the mosque, the executive committees acquired inordinate powers, a situation not characteristic of Islam in Muslim countries.

The executive committees developed constitutions that are "congregational" in character. Usually elected, these committees reserved the rights to hire and dismiss the Imams who do not agree with their policies. Several of the Imams who came from the Middle East showed great reluctance to accept this division of power. (One Imam referred to it as a Papist innovation.)

Islam has no priesthood and no sacraments. The leadership of the congregational prayer is usually reserved for the most learned man in the congregation. Whether that person is one who is most learned in Islamic subjects or one who has academic degrees has been a divisive issue in some mosques.[47]

Imams who have come from the Middle East to serve different communities are versed in the *Qur'an*, *Hadith* and other Islamic subjects,
but sometimes lack empathy for the Canadian realities. They expect
reverence and obedience from the congregation and tend to be satisfied
to exercise the authority of their role without any attempt to persuade
the leadership in the executive committees, who though versed with the
Canadian ways of functioning are not "Islamically aware". Furthermore,
members of the executive committees are very reluctant to relinquish
their powers and tend to have "a built-in skepticism about the Imam."
Imams that have had some education in Canada and the United States
appear to provide the leadership to which some congregations respond
favorably.

The leadership of the Council of Muslim Communities in Canada realizes that some efforts will have to be spent in devising a job description for the Imams. Specified duties include hospital visitation,
counseling, the sharing of responsibility with the executive committee
and the visitation of social clubs and schools as a representative of
the Islamic community. (In fact, the Ottawa Muslim community has ad-
vertized for a teacher-counselor.)

The Islamic community in Canada has not as yet been able to re-
cruit any Arab or Indo-Pakistani young people to go to the Middle East
to study for the imamate. (Three young blacks are studying in the
Middle East.) Meanwhile, several Muslim organizations do not have an
Imam at present including Vancouver, Windsor, Regina and Calgary. The
Egyptian government has promised to supply an Imam for every mosque.
Rabitat al-Alam al-Islami at present pays for three Imams in Canada.
There are several funding agencies besides the Rabitat who at times
have provided help for construction of mosques, for *Qur'ans*, for the
development of educational material and for books on Islam. These include Jamiat al-Falah of Kuwait, Jamiat al-Da'wa of Lybia and al-Majlis
al-A'la li-al-Shu'un al-Islamiyah of Egypt. The existence of these organizations tends to lead some of the people in Canada to depend on
them for funds, while others see in them a danger of dependency and invisible strings of influence and direction.

Only a small number of Muslims attend the mosque on a regular basis. A substantial number attend for the two main feasts (Id al-Adha
and Id al-Fitr). It was reported that about three hundred of a possible
15,000 Muslim Pakistanis attend the main mosque in Toronto for the weekly service. The majority of those who attend are poor, semi-skilled
people who are the victims of prejudice. They are usually conservative

and vocal which gives the religious organization a conservative color-
ing that further alienates the intellectuals and the well-to-do.

Thus the recent immigrants who are the objects of persecution expect the mosque to function as a sect providing a comforting haven and
an insulation from a hostile society, while the acculturated second
generation and the professionals expect it to serve a function similar
to that of the denominational churches of Canada.

Meanwhile, the young generation of Muslims who are in schools are
experiencing the dichotomy between Islamic culture and Western culture.
Many tend to ignore the mosque and the teachings of their parents and
to participate as fully as they can in the mainstream of Canadian culture. The leadership of the Islamic community has become aware that
it cannot passively accept the status quo of accelerated acculturation
among the young and expect to maintain Islam. Consequently, the educational emphasis in the mosques will probably shift from passive receptivity to an active rejection of that which is against the religious
tradition and as such against the will of God. What is being sought is
not the maintenance of an ethnic identity but the projection of a new
world order where all humanity is invited to participate in Islam in
commitment to God, a commitment which would eradicate all ethnic,
national or cultural differences.

Thus the goal is to develop an Islamic identity which is convinced
of the superiority of the Muslim way of life, one that actively advocates the reform of society according to Islamic principles. The goal
is to resist assimilation into the host culture and instead to absorb
and reform it, that it may conform to the religious ideals of Islam.

In his speech to the delegates from over two hundred Islamic congregations this past April Salem Azzam, the Secretary General of the
Islamic Council of Europe said, "The greatest task that besets us in
America and in Europe is not only to conserve our ideological and cultural identity, but also to develop true Islamic character in the individual and establish dynamic Muslim community at the social level. Preservation of the true Islamic tradition and its promotion in this rather
uncongenial atmosphere is the only road to survival and progress. Islam
is not a national ideal, and there is nothing like American Islam, European Islam or Arab Islam. Whatever be the local variations in certain
forms of expression, Islam is one and indivisible."

"The second aspect of the challenge relates to the outside world.
Islam is opposed to the materialistic way of life and wants to

reconstruct human life on the basis of moral principles and eternal
values given by God through His revelation."[48]

Thus the rejection of the materialism and racism of the West is
not seen as a regression or a flight into ethnocentrism; rather, it
must be viewed as an attempt to transcend the "tribalism" of language
and race and as an invitation into theo-centrism. This avenue appears
to be the only option available given the uncompromising commitment to
ideal Islam and the anti-Arab, Anti-Pakistani, Anti-Muslim attitude of
the Canadian society.

Arab Muslims in Canada

Thus far we have seen that the proponents of normative Islam continue to maintain the rejection of the Westernizing forces both in the
Arab world and abroad insisting that one can borrow the technology of
the West without being polluted by its accompanying gods of materialism and secularization. They affirm that Islam as a way of life is
the only viable option for Muslims in North America as well as in the
whole world, and that it does provide the only answer for the moral
and ethical perplexity of Western society.

Meanwhile a relatively small number of Muslims in Canada appear
to be totally committed to the fulfilment of the details of the Islamic law. Between 1%-5% in different cities attend the mosque on a
regular basis. This however should not be seen as a rejection of the
Muslim faith as obsolete, rather it is an adjustment to modernity and
insistence that religion is a personal matter. A much higher per-
centage (in some areas estimated at 70%) of Muslims in Canada fast the
month of Ramadan while many more abstain from eating pork.

Many non-conformist Muslims quoted the phrase *al-din yusrun wala
'usrun* "Religion is for ease and not difficulty" i.e. Islam is not
instituted to make life difficult by imposing restrictions, rather it
is there to aid them in facing the problems of life and in providing
peace of mind and certitude which is necessary for the functioning
of integrated human beings. Others quoted the phrase which says,
"Each person is left to his religion to estimate his needs", i.e. the
decision of whether to borrow money with interest etc...is left to
the individual conscience.

The non-conformist attitude is sanctioned by a century of Muslim
efforts to re-interpret Islam for modern man. Based on the teachings
of Muhammad Abduh and his disciples that a great deal of Islamic law
is an accretion of culturally conditioned interpretations and that

Muslims should be guided only by the *Qur'an* and the practice of the
Prophet, the modernizing efforts have received support among the
educated Westernized and semi-Westernized middle classes of the Arab
world. For them religion provides the psychological certitude of the
possession of truth.

Normative Islam, on the other hand, continues to receive support
from the working classes and the rural inhabitants, especially those
who are at present migrating in record numbers to the cities in search
of better employment. It is from their ranks that al-Azhar continues
to draw most of its students who provide the leadership for the mosques in all parts of the Muslim world.

In order to assess the impact of the Canadian environment on
Arab Muslims, the author interviewed Canadian immigrants from different Arab countries as well as Canadian-born Muslims of Arab origin.
An assessment of the data gathered should emphasize the variety of
responses and experiences that the respondents detailed. However,
for the purposes of this study generalizations will be outlined and a
summary given keeping in mind the Arab heritage as the criterion of
identification and particularization.

What complicates this kind of study is the situation of flux and
uncertainty concerning the concept of Canadian identity in Canada itself. Most Canadians when asked to define their identity, respond in
negative terms - being Canadian is different from being American or
from being a Britisher. Consequently, although most of the respondents identified themselves as Canadians, they shared the Canadian dilemma of trying to provide a positive description of what that meant.
Many were aware of and discussed at length the difference between the
American "melting pot" and Canadian "multiculturalism", with opinion
almost evenly divided on which would be preferable for Canada.

The Muslim Arab response to the Canadian environment appears to
be dependent on factors that are peculiar to the Arabs themselves as
well as those that are particular to the Canadian environment. The
former include the area from which the immigrant came, his country of
origin, whether he was resident in a rural or urban area, his social
class before immigration and the kind of education he had received
prior to his arrival in Canada. It is also contingent on the extent
of Westernization he had been exposed to and had adopted before his
arrival here, the predominant identity in his home country at the time
of emigration, what ideological commitment he had as well as his

physical appearance--whether he is able to pass or whether his Mediterranean features are too pronounced for him to melt into Canadian society.

As for the Canadian factors that influence his response, these include the place of residence in Canada, whether he lives in an Arab ghetto where maintenance of traditional behavior is at a high premium, or in an area where there are other ethnic concentrations and the degree of receptivity they have for members of different groups to participate in their institutions. Mobility within Canada appears to be a factor in hastening Westernization, with those moving repeatedly becoming more aware of their marginality and rootlessness. On the other hand, several reported apathy and isolation as a result of "civilized nomadism".

Syrian, Palestinian and Jordanian Muslims in Canada generally seem to have a closer affinity to Christians from these countries than to Muslims from other Arab countries. This phenomena reflects the regional cultural preferences of the Middle East including what kind of spices are utilized in foods of the different regions, the preferences in entertainment (e.g. regional dialects and songs, folk dancing and ethnic jokes), a shared outlook on the world and a mutual understanding generated from a common experience in both the home country and the Canadian environment.

A careful scrutiny of the data suggests a more significant factor which is highlighted even further when seen in contrast to the situation among immigrants from Egypt and Lebanon. This is the question of identity in the home country before emigration to Canada. Generally speaking, those who emigrated to Canada before the fifties tend to have religion as a primary identity. Among the educated settlers who came in the fifties and sixties, the predominant identity appears to be that of Arab nationalism. This is true mostly among Syrians, Jordanians, Palestinians and Lebanese Muslims. Egyptian Muslims, on the other hand, tend to adhere to an Egyptian identity, preferring regional national cohesion over against the ideals of Arab nationalism as advocated by Nasser.

The proponents of Arab nationalism have succeeded in forging an identity which is not based on lineage or place of birth; rather, it is created through the appropriation of a primarily linguistic identification with a cultural and historical content. Transported to Canada through emigration, this identity is reduced by the host culture to a linguistic characteristic, a communication skill that is obsolete in

some instances and dispensable in most. By the second generation, the
cultural and historical content of the identity becomes hazy and a
source of tension and alienation due to the negative connotation and
ridicule imparted by the host culture.

The recent civil war in Lebanon has created major divisions among
those of Arab background. Not only has it aggrevated the suspicion
between Maronites and Muslims, it has also raised questions about the
adequacy of Arab nationalism as an identity, including the suspicion
by some Muslims of the ability of Arab Christians to share in the
goals and hopes of the Arab world.

Thus we note that regional identities, political commitments and
religious and cultural affiliations of the home countries continue
to play a major role in the cohesion or division of the Arab Muslims
in Canada. This is especially true among members of the first generation, whereas members of the second and third generation are bewilder-
ed and disgusted by all these divisive elements. Many take refuge in
apathy and dissociation as they choose not to grieve over the energies
wasted in the alienating and destructive hostilities in the Arab community.

A great deal of energy is expended in efforts to transcend re-
gionalism, nationalism, factionalism and other divisive factors. Most
respondents agreed that unity is the ideal for which they strive, yet
it appears to be constantly eluding the group. The political struggles and squabbles of the Arab world appear to have a direct relationship to the division of the Arabs in Canada. Meanwhile, of greatest
import for the drive to unity is the hostile host culture and the pro-
Zionist Canadian press. These continue to provide the incentive and
the maintaining power of most organizational efforts. Thus the observ-
er can note that the hope for unity, although based on utilitarian interests and ideological commitments, is, in the last analysis, preserved by negative factors.

This tendency is aggravated by the elitist traditional Canadian
institutions that are perceived as closed to the recent immigrants.
Thus the only area of participation in any power,[49] policy or decision
making role is seen as limited, restricting the opportunities for
leadership roles to cultural and ethnic societies. As a result, the
respondents agreed that personal ambition is the major cause of the
failure of these clubs.

A look at the function of clubs among Arab immigrants shows that
prior to the late forties, most clubs were social, cultural, religious

or ethnic in focus. Muslim clubs were very rare due to the small number of Muslims in Canada.

Events in Canada in the middle forties and an awareness on the
part of Arab Canadians of the ignorance of the Canadian public about
events in the Middle East led to the formation of the Canadian Arab
Friendship League in 1945 in Montreal. The League, headed by Muhammad
Said Massoud began publishing *The Canadian Arab*[50] in May of that year.

The hope of the founders was to raise the consciousness of the
Arab immigrants about the nature of the events in the Middle East, to
combat Zionist propaganda in Canada and to make the immigrants proud
of their heritage. The formation of the State of Israel in 1948 was
a great blow to the group. *The Canadian Arab* ceased publication.
However, there were other efforts at forming clubs mostly for cultural
purposes. Among them are the Syrian Youth Club of Toronto, The Syrian
Canadian Fellowship that published *The Voice* for several years, The
Syrian Canadian Association of Montreal, Canadian Friends of the Middle
East in London, Ontario, The Canadian Moslem Benevolent Association of
the same city, The Lebanese Canadian Society and the Nile Cultural
Club.

The Arab Israeli war of 1967 led to the formation of the Canadian
Arab Federation[51] in the hope of coordinating a response to the pro-
Israeli propaganda in Canada. Its hope was to provide a means of
cooperation for Arab organizations in this country, to defend Arab
rights and to encourage the friendly relations between the Arab and
Canadian communities. The attrition rate of these clubs has been
quite high in recent years due to the variety of backgrounds of the
immigrants who live in the metropolitan areas.[52] Where chain immigration has occurred and the members are related by marriage or come from
the same geographical areas (e.g. the Arab communities of London, Windsor, Calgary and Edmonton) more stable associations have been formed
due to the commitment of a cohesive nucleus.

Regional and ideological commitments are also reflected in the
Middle Eastern papers that are read by the immigrants. These publications are available in most Canadian cities. A substantial number of
immigrants read *al-Ahram* (published in Cairo) because of its comprehensive coverage; however, whereas Egyptians tend to trust its reports,
Syrians pay more attention to *al-Baath*, Iraqis to *al-Thawrah* and Lebanese to *al-Hayat* and *al-Hawadeth*. Periodicals that deal with political, religious and cultural subjects as well as women's magazines are
also available.

A surprising number of recent immigrants own short wave radios on which they can listen to news broadcasts, readings from the *Qur'an* and religious services from the Middle East.[53] The more recent the immigrant, the more anxious he appears to have news of the homeland. There also appears a high correlation between the degree of interest and the crises in the area.

The Canadian Arab Press[54] does not seem to provide for the needs of the immigrants. It tends to reflect a variety of interests and is mostly limited in its coverage. Many respondents were not even aware of its existence. Its reports on news from the Middle East are continually rendered obsolete due to its dependency on the news agencies for its contents. News of Canadian Arabs and their activities are usually presented in "public relations" manner. There is a felt need for a Canadian-Arab ethnic literature.

Some Social Patterns Among Arab Muslims

Canadian laws facilitate the acquisition of immigration visas for those who have relatives in Canada who are willing to sponsor them, a fact that has led to several settlements in places like Calgary, Edmonton and Lac La Biche where the Muslims are related before their arrival in the host country. Inter-marriage among members of the community reinforces their group solidarity and identity. The chain migration appears to lead to a more stable social network among the immigrants while impeding their integration into the host society. The recent immigrants act as the sanctioning agent for the preservation of the customs, values and mores of the home culture.

Recent educated immigrants from the urban areas of the Middle East who have come to settle in Canada on the merit system in the fifties and the sixties do not find the psychological fortitude that chain migration seems to provide. Having experienced the cultural alienation of revolutionary and westernizing Arab countries they seek assimilation into the Canadian culture. This assimilation appears to take place mostly on the professional and intellectual level among the first generation immigrants. Social, emotional, religious and political integration appears to elude most of them.

Unlike the areas where chain migration has occurred, social interaction among the educated immigrants tends to center not on relatives but on an intricate network of friends. Mostly restricted to a nucleus of fellow settlers, these relationships tend to ignore the transcients and the migrants in the group. The aim of this association appears to

be the erection of a social structure that guarantees order, continuity and stability. This network of friends acts as an emotional and
psychological ghetto that affirms personal identity and social solidarity which the suspicious Canadian culture, as well as the earlier
immigrants, fail to provide. Participation in group activities, attendance at club meetings and active contribution to the maintenance
of the group become primary tests of belonging.

The main values of the settlers are similar to those of other
Arabs. They continue to expect female chastity and loyalty. Success
and wealth are displayed through the preparation of elaborate meals
and fancy parties, owning expensive cars, going to restaurants and
clubs and taking vacations in Florida and Arizona. Stressing the importance of the individual, they place a high premium on education for
their young men and women.

It seems, therefore, that ethnic identity has not led to the integration or the integratedness of the Westernized immigrants. Although in most cases they have appropriated the language, clothing,
social relationships and food of the host culture before arriving in
Canada, they are faced by a host culture here that is not willing to
integrate them. Thus, much as he might like to be, the immigrant has
not become simply a Canadian, but rather has joined other hyphenated
identities by being perceived as an Arab-Canadian.

In his frustration, the immigrant shares the marginality of the
second-generation Arab in Canada, leading a life that fluctuates between the two worlds of being and becoming. The new immigrant, however, has a first-hand knowledge of his history, his national identity
and his culture. The problem for the second generation immigrant is
even more intense, for while he still suffers the effects of marginality he no longer has the sense of cultural identity enjoyed by those
more recently arrived. Members of the second generation are faced
with several choices: to reject Canadian society entirely as it seems
to have rejected them, to reject Arab identity and continue to attempt
to become integrated into Canadian society, or to realize the difficulty of these choices and to withdraw from a conscious attempt at
either kinds of identity.[55]

Many second and third generation Arabs are surprised when they
visit the Middle East for the first time. Memories of immigrants are
often arrested in time: they tend to see the Middle East as static,
an image reinforced by much of the stereotypical radio and television
programming of the area. Attempting to be faithful to the heritage,

the immigrant often fails to realize what changes have actually taken place in the home country. One father admitted that when he returned to Lebanon for a visit he realized that he was raising his daughter in Canada in a stricter manner than his relatives overseas.

For most Arab Muslims surveyed there is clearly some change in social patterns. Instead of men and women doing their visiting separately, activities tend to take place in family groupings. Such segregation as there is seems to be natural rather than imposed. The women tend to sit and talk with each other, although even this is changing. Often topics that would be taboo for mixed company in the old country are freely discussed, including sexual references and off-color stories. The older women, while present, pretend not to hear such talk, although the younger ones are more at ease and generally participate freely in the conversation.

Discussions with Arab students on Canadian campuses showed that there is an initial rise in the sense of Muslim identity among this age group upon their arrival in Canada. This is attributed by the students to their shock at Canadian sexual promiscuity as well as such practices as drinking and eating pork. The deepening of Islamic identity takes place at a higher rate among female students who bear the brunt of the preservation of their family honor. Religion offers refuge from the temptations of society. Several students indicated that they now wear long sleeves, cover their hair with a scarf and pray daily, practices they did not observe in their home countries.

Some of the male students agreed that they tend to expect to have sexual relations with the Canadian girls they date and would have no qualms about marrying one who had dated other men. However, all unequivocally asserted that they had no respect for any Arab who is "loose" and that if they married an Arab they would expect her to be a virgin.

Alienation from the host culture of the sort described above apparently has contributed heavily to a kind of ghetto mentality for Muslims in Canada. Nonetheless they welcome converts in to the community of Islam and provide the opportunity for easy assimilation into their religious affiliation. Islam not only motivates the community to seek growth, but provides the cohesiveness to make new members feel that they are a genuine part of the whole. Each convert affirms the validity of the faith, upholds the universalistic aspects of it and confirms its efficacy for life in the new land. Converts who by definition have been part of the Canadian culture, enjoying the security it provides

which may well be envied by the Muslim immigrants, choose through conversion to opt out of that cultural identity and in that very process
to condemn it as in some sense inferior to the new Muslim identity.
In this they support the faith of the elder Muslim immigrants that
what they have preserved is inherently right, legitimating their desire to show their youth that the cultural patterns of Canada to which
they might be tempted are in fact inferior.

Attempts to reduce the religious law in Islam to the realm of customs have met with some success in secularizing and Westernizing Arab
countries. For this process, Islam has paid a price, that of the commitment of the young people to nationalism and/or socialism. This
solution has been repeatedly challenged by the Muslim Brotherhood and
other Muslims who see in it the rejection of the fundamental teaching
of Islam. It is difficult at present to speculate whether the West
will produce a Canadian Islam or whether adherence to the religious
law will become more prevalent. The next two generations of Canadian
born Muslims may provide the answer depending on the leadership input
from the Muslim countries and the rate of immigration of new committed
Muslims.

FOOTNOTES

1 Abu Laban, Baha, "The Arab Canadian Community" in Hagopian and
   Paden, *The Arab Americans: Studies in Assimilation* (Wilmette,
   Illinois: 1969); Barclay, Harold B., "An Arab Community in Lac La
   Biche, Alberta," *Anthropologica*, Spring 1968; Barclay, H. B.,
   "Perpetuation of Muslim Tradition in the Canadian North," *The Mus-
   lim World*, January 1969; Fathi, Asghar, "Mass Media and a Moslem
   Immigrant Community in Canada," *Anthropologica*, Vol. XV, #2, 1973;
   Khattab, A. M., "The Assimilation of Arab Muslims in Alberta,"
   (M. A. Thesis) University of Alberta, 1969 (A summary of the thesis
   was published under the same title in *Islam Canada*, Vol. 1, #2,
   July 1972); Wolf, C. U., "Muslims in the American Mid-West," *The
   Muslim World*, January 1960.

2 Massoud, Muhammad Said, *I Fought as I Believed* (Toronto: 1976,
   p. 5). There may have been several individuals who came to Canada
   earlier. Census Canada for 1871 shows that there were 13 Muslims
   in the country that year. However, the census for 1881 and 1891
   lists their number as zero. This could be accounted for by the
   fact that some of the early immigrants returned to Lebanon and that
   others tended to travel back and forth between the United States
   and Canada.

3 Harney, Robert F. and Troper, Harold, *Immigrants* (Toronto: 1975)
   p. V.

4 Abu Laban, *op. cit.*, p. 31.

5 There are no official figures on the number of Muslims in Canada.
   The Council of Muslim Communities in Canada is in the process of
   conducting a census. The figures quoted in the text were given
   to the author by the Secretary of the Council and were corroborated
   by several Muslim leaders in different cities. cf. Hamdani, D. H.,
   "Spirit of Islam: Economic Stabilization and Political Participation," *Islam Canada*, June 1977, Vol. 5, #2, pp. 5-7.

6 *Islam Canada*, Vol. 1, #2, July 1972, p. 11.

7 Muinuddin, M. "Canadian Muslims in a Multicultural Setting," *Islam
   Canada*, Vol. 5, #1, May 1977, p. 8; cf. *Islam Canada*, Vol. 1, #1,
   June 1972.

8 See footnote #5.

9 These include the Druze, considered as unorthodox sectarians by
   Sunni Muslims. Their tendency to practice *taqiyyah* (dissimulation)
   can be seen in Canada. Some participate with the Sunnis in the
   mosque service (as in Edmonton and other parts of Canada); H. S.
   Massoud placed one of the corner stones of the New London Mosque in
   1961 and delivered a speech at the founding ceremony. (See *I
   Fought as I Believed*, p. 375). Mr. Massoud's brother became an
   active member of the Greek Orthodox Church (the Arab congregation).

10   Muhammad Mosque on Cote des Neiges in Montreal and Muhammad Mos-
     que on Eglington Avenue in Toronto.

11   Many graduates from North American universities have opted to set-
     tle in the United States and Canada. They have formed the Associ-
     ation of Muslim Social Scientists, The Islamic Medical Association
     of North America and the Islamic Scientists and Engineers of North
     America. (Several members of the CMCC executive board were mem-
     bers of MSA during their student days).

12   *Islam Canada*, Vol. 5, #2, June 1977, p. 8.

13   It should be noted that Rabitat al-Alam al-Islami tends to be a
     conservative body with a defined outlook on what is the "Islamic
     way of life." It was established in the early sixties by the
     Saudi government to combat the influence of Nasser and Islamic
     Socialism on communities all over the Islamic world.

14   *Islam Canada*, Vol. 5, #1, May 1977, p. 15. (The Organization of
     the Islamic Conference with headquarters in Jeddah, Saudi Arabia,
     tends to be less politically oriented than the Rabitat. It is
     an inter-governmental agency interested in the world-wide communi-
     ties of Islam).

15   *Islam Canada* is published monthly by the CMCC, beginning June 1972.
     Publication was suspended for several years due to financial dif-
     ficulties, resuming in 1977. The policy of the magazine is
     (a) "To present the Islamic way of life as defined by the Quran
     and Sunnah.
     (b) To strengthen the bonds of brotherhood among the Muslim com-
     munities and among individual Muslims.
     (c) To promote and encourage mutual appreciation and friendly
     relations between Muslims and non-Muslims.
     (d) To stimulate Islamic thinking and action among Muslim communi-
     ties in the North American setting."

16   The individual exceptions include Ali Abd al-Raziq who wrote *Usul
     al-Hukm* (Foundations of Government) in 1926. In it he maintained
     that the ideal was not practical, because it could not be imple-
     mented. He therefore called for the separation of religion and
     state. He was unanimously condemned for un-Islamic thinking, his
     ideas being rejected by the conferences of Cairo in 1926, of Mecca
     in 1926, of Jerusalem in 1931 and of Geneva in 1935 - all convened
     to deal with the crisis generated by the abolition of the Cali-
     phate, all asserting the necessity of a Caliph, but all ineffectual
     because they could not agree on who would assume the office nor the
     scope of his powers.

          In recent years, the controversy has shifted to the articles
     of constitution in different Muslim countries, eg. Colonel Qadafi
     of Lybia championing the Islamic nature of the state, while the
     socialist regimes of Syria, Iraq, Algeria and Egypt (until 1971)
     were downplaying its importance.

          For a translation of some of the contemporary arguments on the
     question see CENAM REPORTS 2/73, *Controversy, Dialogue and the New
     Arab Man*, (Beirut: 1973) pp. 1-22.

17   In many homes of Muslims of Lebanese origin throughout Canada, pic-
     tures of Nasser decorate the walls along with Quranic verses.

18 This abuse originated in the capitulations which conceded to
    France the right to protect Catholic subjects of the Sultanate.
    Similar rights were granted by later Sultans to Russia to pro-
    tect Greek Orthodox subjects and to Britain to protect Jews and
    Protestants. This gave foreign powers the excuse to interfere
    in the internal affairs of the Ottoman Empire.

19 In many Muslim countries working hours are altered and restric-
    tions on the sale and consumption of food and beverages are
    strictly enforced to assist believers in the fulfilment of the
    religious duty of fasting the month of Ramadan.

20 The long days of the summer months in North America have produced
    several dispensations concerning the fast. One legal opinion for
    residents in Newfoundland permits fasting for twelve hours of the
    day. Another opinion calls on Muslims in North American to syn-
    chronize the duration of the fast with that of Mecca.

21 Both Mawdudi in 1974 and Nadawi in 1977 lectured to Islamic com-
    munities throughout Canada affirming the ban on receiving or pay-
    ing interest. Cf. *Islam Canada*, Vol. 2, #6, July-August 1974.

22 *Islam Canada*, Vol. 1, #5, October 1972.

23 Accommodation to Canadian realities is also given as the reason
    for the purchase of insurance for cars, homes and even mosques.
    Muslim religious leaders from overseas on lecture tours in Canada
    have condemned the practice as a faithless act and a demonstration
    of lack of trust in God's providence.

24 To deal with this problem some Muslims have opted to distribute
    any interest received on investments as tithe. This practice was
    condemned by Mawdudi who said that it compared "to the action of a
    pickpocket who gives money so obtained to charity." For a full
    text of his opinions on the subject see "Al-Maududi: Guidelines
    for Islamic Living", *Islam Canada*, Vol. 2, #6, July-August 1974,
    pp. 4-6.

25 *Bulletin of the Islamic Center*, Washington, D. C., Vol. 2, #3,
    August 1973, pp. 14-15.

26 Some explain the eating of cheese through the Islamic legal posi-
    tion of *istihala* (to change from one form to another) used to per-
    mit the consumption of vinegar which was originally wine.

27 Writing of wills is very rare in Muslim countries. To protect the
    rights of the beneficiaries, Islamic law allows the individual to
    will one third of his wealth in the manner he sees fitting. The
    rest is divided according to an established formula.

28 Divorce is not as big a threat in Canada as it is in the home coun-
    try where it continues to be utilized as an assertion of male domi-
    nance. References to it crop up often in conversation, mostly as a
    joke.

29 According to Islamic law, any child nine years or older is placed
    in custody of the father. Younger children can remain with the
    mother until they reach the age of nine.

30 Islamic law provides a specific sum as settlement at the time of
    divorce, the amount of which is agreed upon and documented in the
    marriage contract.

31 In seeking divorce in Ontario, men are advised to claim committing
    adultery in order to speed the legal proceedings, this being the
    only loophole to the requirement of the three-year separation
    period.

32 Sura 4:34. "Men are the protectors of women, because God has
    given the one precedence over the other because of their support
    of them from their wealth."

33 The *Qur'an* allows Muslim males to marry more than one wife. One
    Muslim pointed out that the prohibition on multiple marriages in
    Canada can be circumvented by the application of Canadian common
    law.

34 Annual meetings of the Muslim Student Association provide the op-
    portunity for Muslim college students to meet members of the other
    sex and contract marriage. Periodically one can find advertise-
    ments for marriage partners in some magazine. The June 1975 is-
    sue of the *Bulletin/Newsletter* of the Islamic Center of Quebec
    carried an ad for a Muslim marriage bureau named "Sincere Youth
    Services" in St. Laurent, Quebec.

35 Several Muslims expressed the belief that the time for sex educa-
    tion is the period between engagement and marriage.

36 *Bulletin/Newsletter*, June 1975.

37 At the Croatian Islamic Center in Toronto about seventy five peo-
    ple attend the Sunday prayers. Of these between three and five
    are Croation and about ten to fifteen are Arab. The rest are
    Indo-Pakistani. A study by C. U. Wolf of Muslims in Windsor in
    1960 showed that Albanian and Yugoslav Muslims do not mix socially
    with the Arabs. See "Muslims in the American Mid-West" *The Muslim
    World*, January 1960, Vol. L, #1, pp. 39-48.

38 Ethnic preferences for certain mosques appear in Muslim countries.
    As one Imam explained, Islam has no restrictions on the building
    of mosques as places of worship (*masjid*) or who utilizes them;
    however, each city must have one large mosque as a place of gath-
    ering (*jami*) where all Muslims congregate on feast days and other
    important occasions to affirm their solidarity, brotherhood and
    commitment to the unitivity of God.

39 For Indo-Pakistani Muslims the use of English for the dissemina-
    tion of Islamic teaching is not a recent phenomenon. Numerous
    publications have appeared in that language in the last three
    decades.

40 In Toronto, there are some members of the Jami mosque who want
    their children to learn Urdu instead of Arabic so that they might
    be able to understand their heritage. This was viewed with sus-
    picion by other members of the mosque.

41 Islamic education was given the highest priority by the leadership
    surveyed. An editorial in *Islam Canada*, Vol. 3, #4, January 1975,

p. 3, calls for the allocation of 25-50% of "annual budgets to Islamic education of adults and youth - born Muslims, new Muslims and non-Muslims. If they do not comprehend the broader perspectives of Islamic education, they may be only fooling themselves."

42 Islamic practice allows communal prayer (*salat al-jamaa*) at designated times where only one sermon is preached. In the Friday prayer (*salat al-Juma*) two sermons are preached.

43 Kenny, L. M. "The Middle East in Canadian Social Science Textbooks" *Arabs in America: Myths and Realities* by B. Abu Laban and F. T. Zeadey (Wilmette, Ill: 1975), p. 138.

44 A few years ago, several mosques allowed some folk dancing in the basement. This was ruled as objectionable by Imams from the Middle East. It is now the consensus that people can gather, consume food and socialize at the mosque, but that no dancing will be tolerated.

45 In the Arab world, older women attend prayers at the mosque. This is not true about Muslim women in India and Pakistan. (The exception is in the state of Kerala in India where women participate in the Friday prayer as a result of the Wahabi revival).

46 The mosque in Calgary and that of Edmonton face Northeast (instead of the usual Southeast) that being computed as the shortest distance to Mecca.

47 *Bulletin/Newsletter*, February 1976, p. 4; *Bulletin/Newsletter*, September-October 1973.

48 "Challenge to Islam" *Islam Canada*, June 1977, Vol. 5, #2, p. 4. A similar attitude is voiced by S. S. Mufassir, "After Two Hundred Years: Islam is Taking Roots in America" *Islamic Items*, Vol. 4, #39, p. 2, where he says that Muslims in America "are not involved with creating a 'nationalist Islam' or 'American Islam' but simply and purely ISLAM, the universal way of life for all human beings."

49 Muslims appear to shy away from political participation in Canada. The only exception appears to be Larry Schabin of High River who was elected a member of the Provincial Legislature in Edmonton. He is a Progressive Conservative.

50 Massoud, *I Fought as I Believed*, pp. 13, 17.

51 In its 1977 convention in Montreal, the Federation listed as its members the following clubs and associations: The Canadian Arab Club of Calgary; The Canadian Arab Friendship Association of Edmonton; The Arab Community Center of Hamilton; The Canadian Arab Society of London; The Canadian Arab Association, and The Palestine Arab Association of Montreal; Le Comite Palestine de L'Universite Laval in Quebec; The Canadian Arab Club of Sudbury; The Arab Palestinian Association; The Arab Association in Toronto; The Canada-Palestine Solidarity Association; and The Canadian Arab Friendship Association of Vancouver; and The Canadian Arab Federation in Windsor.

52 The 1976 elections of the executive committee of the Canadian Arab Association of Montreal reflected the sources of tension in the

group. The board was composed of two Lebanese, two Egyptians and
one each from Syria, Palestine and Iraq. Since then the club has
gone into receivership due to the internal hostilities and the
community's lack of support.

53   Those interviewed in Montreal, Toronto and Calgary corroborated
the findings of Asghar Fathi in Western Canada. See "Mass Media
and a Moslem Immigrant Community in Canada" *Anthropologica*, Vol.
XV, 1973, pp. 201-230.

54   The Arab Canadian press includes the following publications: *Al-
Uruba*, trilingual published by the Society of Arab Students in
Montreal; *Arab Dawn*, trilingual published in Ste-Foy, Quebec;
The Arab World Review, trilingual, in Montreal; *Canadian Middle
East Journal*, trilingual, in Montreal; *Al-Ittihad*, English quar-
terly, published by the Muslim Student Association in the US and
Canada; *Arab Canada Newsletter*, English, in Ottawa; *Asda Marakah*,
Arabic, London; *Ash Sharara*, English, Montreal; *Fedayin*, bilingual,
Montreal; *Jerusalem Times*, English-Arabic, Vancouver; *News from
Iraq*, Arabic, Ottawa; *The Source*, Arabic-English, Edmonton; *Islam
Canada*, English, Toronto; *Bulletin/Newsletter*; English, Montreal;
Weekly Bulletin, English, Toronto; *The Muslim Star*, published by
the Federation of Islamic Associations in the US and Canada.

55   Material on the condition of the second generation is very rare to
find. Two exceptions are: Henny Hassan "The Second Generation
Arabs" (typescript) which the author read at *The Canadian Arab
Heritage Conference*, London, Ontario, November 1976, and Amain
Kadrie "The Dilemma of the Canadian Arab Youth" read at the same
conference.

THE MUSLIM EXPERIENCE IN CANADA

Another paper in this conference deals with the population, ethnic composition, history, various organizations of Muslims in Canada.
In this presentation I wish to discuss some select issues of adaptation and assimilation of Arab - Lebanese Muslims to the Canadian context. Let us first bear in mind that we are here concerned with a
community that has grown by enormous strides only in the last three
decades. This means that the vast majority of Muslims in Canada are
foreign born and the second and third generations are in a distinct
minority. Thus this is a minimally assimilated community. Secondly,
the Muslims are almost entirely of Afro-Asiatic extraction. They
share cultures which are more divergent than most of the other ethnic
communities in Canada. Thus, religion aside, assimilation may be expected to be a more arduous task. Thirdly, it might be argued that
Muslims in Canada should experience more difficulties than other immigrants in adapting to a new and non-Muslim socio-cultural milieu since
Islam is a highly rigid and legalistic religious system which imposes
such specific requirements on its adherents as to allow for little
flexibility or adjustment to varying cultural conditions. History
shows this notion of Islam to be at best a half truth. It is true that
Islam is quite specific and dogmatic in many of its prescriptions and
is no doubt more legalistic than most of the other world religions.
However, Muslims have demonstrated that the system is malleable; they
have moved into an immense variety of different cultural environments
and have managed to adapt their religion to them or the environment to
the religion.

Another point to bear in mind in connection with the immigration
of Muslims to non-Muslim lands such as North America is that there may
be a selective process at work in which the more marginal Muslims, the
less committed to Islam, are more willing to give up the security of
the Muslim world for the attractions of the unbelieving world. I have
no data to demonstrate this explicitly but I present it as a hypothesis which should not be ignored in considering the religiosity and
adaptation of the Muslim immigrants to Canada.

Finally we should note that Muslim immigration to North America
has been from culturally heterogeneous zones of the Muslim world. The
Lebanese and Albanians are from areas which have traditionally been

highly mixed religious communities where there has been continual
association between Christian and Muslim communities of moreorless
the same size. The other major ethnic group among Muslims, the Indo-
Pakistani, has a background of Hindu-Muslim interaction and of nearly
two centuries of British-Christian influence and interference. The
Yugoslavian Muslims are from an area where the Muslims have been a
minority among Christians. Therefore almost all Muslims in Canada are
from ethnic groups which have a considerable exposure to multi-reli-
gious experience. We might predict then on this basis that the adaptation to the Canadian milieu might be easier than say for a devout
Muslim from Saudi Arabia or Morocco.

     Having said all this I do not mean to suggest that the lot of the
Muslim immigrant to Canada is an easy one or as easy as that of a Norwegian or a Ukrainian. Because of their espousal of Islam Muslim immigrants do have special problems not shared by others. Islam does after all inhibit assimilation to a Christian Canadian context. What I
have been trying to suggest is that the particular kinds of people who
choose to be immigrants to this country make the inevitable process of
adaptation and assimilation simpler. Before proceeding I wish to
stress that most of the problems of adaptation are not peculiar to the
Muslim immigrant in Canada; they are often problems of the entire Muslim community in a rapidly changing world. The behavior of Canadian
Muslims may in fact not be that deviant from their brethren in the
Middle East. Now let us consider specific problems of Muslim adaptation.

The Immigrant and the "Pillars of the Faith"

     One very relevant issue concerns personal ritual--the performance
of the socalled pillars of the faith. As most everyone knows Muslims
are obligated to perform a personal litany or "prayer" several times
each day. This *salat* however, is faithfully observed by a minority
of Muslims even in Muslim lands. Nevertheless, these lands provide
a cultural milieu which encourages the performance of this ritual, a
milieu which is clearly lacking in Canada. Thus, in the Middle East
it is in no way unusual to see men bowing in the *salat* in the street
or on the sidewalk. There are also many available mosques; there is
the regular call to prayer, *and* places of business allow time off for
the rite. Then, too, there is inducement to pray because so many
others do it.

My experience both in the Middle East and among Canadian Muslims leads me to suspect that the *salat* is practiced less among the latter and I would attribute this not only to the above environmental factors but also to the possibility as mentioned above that the immigrants are more marginal Muslims.

The Friday noon prayer is established as the regular weekly congregational service in Islam. Here the regular *salat* is performed by a group who follow the prostrations of a prayer leader and is accompanied by a sermon. In Canada of course Friday is a regular work day inhibiting attendance. As a result Muslims have accommodated to the Christian pattern by holding their *jama'a* (congregational service) on Sunday noon, often following after a "Sunday School".

Another ritual obligation of Muslims is the fast of Ramadan. In most of the Arab world the fast is observed far more commonly and widely than the regular observance of the *salat*. Family and community life in a Muslim village for example is wholly reorganized to adapt to Ramadan. There is the force of total social commitment to the fast so that the non-faster in persona non grata. Transferred to a Christian context such as Canada where few at all are fasting, where most never even heard of Ramadan, and there is certainly no catering to it, one has a situation conducive to ignoring the ritual. Thus, in Canada while observance of the feast which celebrates the end of the month of Ramadan is widespread among Muslims, the actual adherence to thirty days of fasting is a practice of only a small number of devotees.

A third major pillar of Islam is alms giving and as in the rest of the Muslim world today this ritual has been individualized so that a person may give aid to the needy at his own discretion. The pilgrimage to Mecca, a final major obligatory ritual is rarely performed by Canadian Muslims, but we must remember that only a small minority of Muslims even in Africa or Asia ever attain the title of Bajji.

The Immigrant and Other Important Tenets of Islam

Two food taboos are considered crucial to correct Muslim behavior. One is the prohibition of alcoholic beverages and the other of pork. The latter is almost universally observed and it is uncommon to find a Canadian Muslim eating pork, but the drinking of the liquor is more readily accepted and practiced. This follows a general trend elsewhere in the Muslim world. One finds especially among the upper and middle classes large numbers who will drink alcohol and in some Muslim countries (e.g., the Sudan) the practice is common among all classes.

Inheritance regulations in Islam are very precise in stating how a legacy should be divided among the heirs. These regulations make provision for division of the property among the descendents and relatives of the deceased, prohibiting favoritism, although awarding any given male twice as much as a female. In Canada Muslims must prepare wills in order to insure Muslim inheritance.

A major facet of Muslim teaching concerns the family, marriage and the role of women. Much of the practice relating to marriage and family reflects prevailing Muslim attitudes towards women. They are conceived as subordinate to men, as reflecting the honor and good name of the kin group to which they belong. Thus husbands are deemed protectors and guides of their wives; fathers and brothers as overseers of daughters and sisters. Women must act in a circumspect manner and always be on guard against the possibility of compromising family honor. Women's "rights" however do exist, but they are more limited than those in the Western world. However, it might be noted that women in the Muslim world do not ordinarily adopt their husband's name on marriage but retain their own and a woman also has the right to hold and dispose of her own property.

Two aspects of Islamic family and marriage law are adversely affected by Canadian regulations. These include the permission of polygamy--as many as four wives at one time--by Islam and the Muslim divorce regulations which make it extremely easy for a man to divorce his wife and very difficult for a woman to divorce her husband. The Canadian law against polygamy does not actually have much negative affect on local Muslims. Few Muslims anywhere have more than one wife. In most Muslim countries between one and ten percent of all married males are polygamous. Further, modern Muslim states are placing increasing restrictions on marriage. Both Turkey and Tunisia have outlawed polygamy and Egypt has crubed the practice.

Divorce regulations are a different matter. In Canada a man cannot so easily divorce his wife and further since the process entails quite an expense there are men who remain married--often separated from their wives--who in the Muslim land of their origin would have long since divorced. But the chief concern of the Muslim male regarding Canadian divorce law and probably the major deterrent to divorce is the custom of awarding children to the wife where Islamic law being patrilineally oriented gives children by age seven to the husband.

Although it is not a religious regulation Arab Muslims do prefer marriage to father's brother's daughter and other "first" cousins.

This is technically illegal in Canada being considered incest. The
practice however exists among Arab immigrants.

The Muslim family is patriarchal giving priority to the senior
male in the household. In Canada the Muslim immigrant is confronted
with a different perspective which emphasizes a greater equality in
decision making among the family members especially between husband and
wife. The immigrant is faced with widespread notions of permissiveness
towards the young, and of youths participating in family decision making. Schools, mass media and other communication institutions spread
the values of the democratic system, of sexual equality and the eleva-
tion of youth. The more widespread assumption of authority and power
positions by women in Canadian society adds to the undermining of the
superior role of the male. Patriarchal authority is further reduced as
the Muslim's own wife assumes more responsibility in the home since the
husband is away working for most of the day. It is reduced as well by
the fact that the male head no longer has sufficient economic power to
command the obedience of family members and he cannot turn to kinsmen
for support since this group too is weakened and impotent. These problems it should be noted are also increasingly important issues in the
Muslim world as a whole as people leave the agrarian village way of
life for a more urbanized one.

A major point of stress in the family of the Canadian Muslim is in
the role of the daughter. The traditionally appropriate pattern requires the daughter to be retiring and modest. Dating, particularly
the practice of a young man and a girl going off some place alone, is
unheard of as is the practice of boys and girls dancing as single couples and unchaperoned. In Canada all of this is changed. There is
great social pressure from high school on to "date" and to attend school
dances. Parents find it extremely difficult or impossible to control
their daughters in what they think is the correct behavior. Not only
is the fact that all neighbors and fellow students indulge in these
practices but also a girl can more readily defy her parents by seeking
employment and financial independence.

Another related crucial problem concerns mate selection. Here
again the traditional view of marriage as a contract between families
not individuals leads to an emphasis on parental control and mate selection, but in Canada the doctrines of individual choice and romantic
love prevail. "An expression often heard from members of the second
generation when opposed by their parents, especially in matters of marriage and mate selection, is 'I am in a free country'" (Khattab, 39).

In Canada one of the greatest fears a Muslim father may have is
that his daughter will marry a non-Muslim. Islamic law allows a man
to marry a woman who adheres to one of the "religions of the book"
(Judaism, Christianity or Zoroastrianism), but a Muslim woman may not
marry outside the faith. The more conservative Muslim may in fact oppose even the marriage of a man to a non-Muslim on the basis of his
practical experience, holding that the children of such a marriage will
be influenced by their mother and her kin and there will be an immense
temptation to abjure Islam or at least become a very poor Muslim.
Thus, there are very strong sanctions against exogamous marriage.
These sanctions are effective in so far as Muslims live concentrated in
sufficiently large communities with minimal contacts with non-Muslims
and in so far as individuals accept the practice of arranging marriages
with girls in Lebanon (very common among the first generation Lebanese
born). However as the number of the second and third generation increases and as Muslims move out of ethnic neighborhoods to disperse
throughout the country there can not help but be a break down in the
endogamous practice. My own investigations in Edmonton and Lac La
Biche indicate that thus far the great majority of marriages are endogamous, but those which are not are primarily among second and third
generation people.

Feasts and rites of passage appear to be greatly attenuated in
length of time and in investment in food and gifts in Canada. The
circumcision of boys anywhere between age two and seven is accompanied
in the Muslim world by rather elaborate feasts and celebration. In
Canada the common practice of circumcising boys in the hospital shortly
after birth acts as a deterrent to these festivities.

Children are usually given Muslim names, but these are invariably
adapted to European sounding names so that Muhammad becomes Mike or
Mickey, Abd al Alla becomes Albert, Atta becomes Otto. Surnames are
only a recent innovation in the Middle East and most adopt their lineage name or the given name of their paternal grandfather as a surname
and this too may be Anglicized. A Lebanese who was for many years prominent in the political and social affairs of the Northwest Territories
bore the surname Baker, a translation of his Arabic name, Farrān. Because of confusion at the immigration depot, inadequate knowledge of
writing English and especially of transliterating it from Arabic, two
brothers or paternal first cousins may sometimes have different appear-
ing surnames. Thus: Fayad and Fyith, Awad and Awid, Charkaoui, Char-
kawi, and Al Sharkawi.

Weddings are rarely more than one day celebrations where in the Middle East they lasted for three days to a week. The *mahr* or bride wealth has in most cases become merely perfunctory. Funerals are followed by a communal gathering but they are no longer the prolonged affairs of the old country. There have been occasional misunderstandings and problems regarding burial. Muslim tradition requires that the deceased be buried on the day he dies; it proscribes both embalming and cremation.

The two great annual Muslim feasts are traditionally accompanied by the sacrifice of a sheep or goat by each family and the distribution of part of the meat to the poor. In Canada this practice has largely been abandoned as Muslims adapt the feasts to more Christmas-like affairs giving gifts especially to children in the family.

In general it is obvious that on moving to Canada most of the color has been removed from the rites of passage and major feasts of Muslims. But again this is not that different from similar changes which occur in the Middle East as Muslims move from the village to the city or, more commonly, as they move into the upper classes.

Accommodation to Specifically Christian Contexts

Examples of accommodation to the Christian environment of Canada have already been mentioned. Some further exploration of this issue would seem to be in order. Canadian Muslims find themselves immersed in what to them is a predominantly Christian milieu. This is especially the case for younger children who in school are among other things daily part of a group which recites the Lord's prayer. More widespread are the Christmas festivities which can be a source of some disturbance to Muslims, although many, like their upper class co-religionists in Cairo and Beirut, purchase and decorate Christmas trees during this season. The more well-to-do Muslims, especially, accommodate to such activities by noting that Jesus is a Muslim prophet and that the Lord's prayer has nothing specifically of Christian doctrine in it. It is sometimes remarked that "We all worship the same God". Indeed for some, Islam is portrayed to the (non-Muslim) interviewer as a kind of unitarian Christianity wherein the primary difference between the two religions concerns the role and nature of Jesus: Islam holding that Jesus was a mortal man and a prophet of a God who is one indivisible supreme being, Christianity attributing divinity to Jesus and dividing the Godhead into three parts.

It is my strong impression that the most "ecumenically" oriented
of Muslims in Canada are those who are the more successful business men
and individuals involved in community affairs. They have among other
things a vested interest in getting along and being accepted by the
larger Christian community and thus in toning down and de-emphasizing
distinctive Muslim teachings and practices. Certainly it is true that
the more "Canadianized", the more assimilated, are the least rigid in
their interpretation of Muslim doctrine and their practice of its rituals, the most accommodating to the Christian context and the most
eager to play down Muslim-Christian differences. The strictest Muslims
tend to be the less assimilated, the less "sophisticated" from a Euro-
Canadian point of view. Unfortunately, it is the latter group which
would be most disturbed by all the Christian exposure in the Canadian
public school system, but it is this group as well which due to the
lack of sophistication in this system, is least aware of this threat to
the Islamic teaching of their young and also unaware of means to combat the threat. The more assimilated as I have suggested are aware and
know also how to combat it, but are uninterested in doing so.

Canadians and Their Attitudes Towards Muslims

An important aspect of the adaptation of any minority group to a
new milieu is the attitude of the more indigenous, dominant population
to the minority. I have no data derived from any systematic investigations to indicate what these attitudes might be concerning the Muslims,
but can offer some impressions.

Lebanese, Syrians and Palestinians do not look physically different from Italians or other south Europeans and have as a result not
suffered from specifically racial conflicts in Canadian society. Egyptians, on the other hand, and particularly the Indo-Pakistanis are
frequently much darker in complexion and consequently have been the
brunt of racial strife.

Aside from the racial issue, world affairs have a way of affecting
attitudes towards immigrant groups as Japanese and Germans know only
too well. Muslims, Arabs and Middle Easterners are still often identified as Turks and Turks identified as murderers of the Muslims in Canada, respect has been built up for their dedication to work, their self
reliance and their ability to adjust to the Canadian scene.

The Means of Maintaining the Tradition

Muslim immigration into Canada is like depositing so many Islamic
droplets into a sea of unbelief. It is extremely difficult to

perpetuate one's religious tradition especially when most of the immigrants themselves are not that well versed in the tradition, and when
so many can be said to be marginally religious. Further so much of
Islamic tradition is perpetuated by reliance on the force of shame,
that is, by an atmosphere of communal participation which is certainly
difficult to generate when one's group is both few in number and scattered.

What are the specific techniques which maintain the tradition in
Canada? First, it is to be noted that immigration is a continuing af-
fair. The older immigrants and their descendants are continually re-
vitalized by a flow of newcomers who remind them of the old ways and
reinforce them. To a less extent, but one of recent importance, is
the greater ease of travel back to the old homeland to visit relatives,
and reinvigorate one's ties in this way. Thus ethnicity reinforces
religion.

Fathi has noted the degree to which Arab immigrants maintain ties
via short wave radio listening so that mass society techniques of communication operate as devices to preserve ethnic enclaves in a so-
called mass society (Fathi, 1973).

Of more importance is the need to have a supply of individuals
formally trained in the Islamic doctrine who devote themselves to teaching and preaching. There is not a single Muslim seminary in the western
hemisphere so that such individuals must be trained overseas. The
Egyptians have been the most generous in providing Muslim clerics to
the immigrant Arab communities in Canada, but there are still not enough
of them. And on occasion the introduction of these individuals into
the immigrant community has been a source for conflict. A newly arrived
imam (prayer leader) is invariably both more conservative and at the
same time more sophisticated and learned in Islamic teaching so that
while he may upbraid the women for wearing flimsy bathing suits he may
also upbraid the men for misguided beliefs that Islam is opposed to
birth control or does not allow women to enter the mosques.

The presence of an *imam* in a community is an essential prerequi-
site to planning community religious education, but also important is
the need for halls or mosques in which to gather and which can act as
symbols and foci of activity.

The perpetuation of the Arabic language (at least the classical
Arabic) is essential to the preservation of Islam as it is now conceived since it is still viewed as only proper that the Quran be read
in Arabic and the prayers be recited in that language as well. A

universal problem in Islam shared by the English speaking Canadian Muslim, the Urdu speaking Pakistani or any of the five hundred million non-Arab Muslims is that adequate comprehension of the Quran hinges upon understanding a foreign language--classical Arabic. Thus, training in language becomes of central importance in the mosque schools. The linguistic issue creates its own problem in terms of assimilation. The Arabic language is closely identified with Islam so that as the Arab moves to greater assimilation in the English-speaking Canadian milieu he sloughs off the Arabic language and in so doing may also be sloughing off the religion as well. This same problem would not arise in the case of Indo-Pakistani Muslims, where the native tongue is one thing, Urdu, i.e. the religious tongue another, Arabic.

Another device for perpetuating the religious tradition is the integration and consolidation of all believers into a single national denominational entity coordinating, among other things, a system of education and publication. The Ismaili followers of the Agha Khan have, like their brethren elsewhere, a truly denominational or sectarian organization with local branches articulated with regional organizations and these in turn with a central organization. Among the Sunnis such an integrated structure is weak and particularly hampered by inter-ethnic conflicts, occurring chiefly between Arabs and Pakistanis. The Sunnis in their past history have invariably been in a position of dominance, rarely, as in Canada, in the stratus of a tiny minority sect. Therefore they have been slow to develop organizational devices for coping in that status.

Multiculturalism and the Muslim Experience in Canada

Canada has been called a multi-cultural country. Presumably this means a nation-state in which several different ways of life are pursued and, if we accept government definitions, it means further that individuals are free to pursue their own cultural traditions and that no one culture is held to be superior over another. I would argue that such a multi-cultural society is a myth and the Muslim example demonstrates this argument. In Canada Muslims are in no sense free to practice their traditional religious law. Polygamy and divorce Muslim style are prohibited. The forces of the establishment speak loudly and clearly against the doctrine of male priority, of seniority by virtue of age, of the patriarchal family, of arranged marriages, and the belief that marriages are contracts between groups and not individuals.

The Arab-Middle Eastern preference for FBD marriage is considered in-
cestuous.

A truly multi-cultural society is impossible given the nature of
the nation-state which demands a high degree of conformity and uniformity particularly in what might be called its structural core. In any
culture, as Linton long ago noted, there are certain universals or
compulsory elements shared by all. Then there are alternatives shared
by a smaller segment and individual peculiarities characteristic of
specific individuals (Linton, 272-4). It is in the realm of the alternatives and individual peculiarities that multiculturalism might be
tolerated. Indeed, the Muslim world itself can provide some of the
best examples of experiments in multiculturalism, the latest one having
been the millet system under the Ottoman Turkish Empire. In modern
times even South Africa is another kind of multicultural experiment.

Canada, within very narrowly circumscribed limits, has multicultural characteristics. At least it is an heterogeneous society with
two clearly dominant cultures. Canadian multiculturalism operates within the limit of a broadly Christian context; it operates as well within the limit of a western European--either French or English--pattern
of family and political organization and within the more universal
pattern of international capitalism as far as the economy is concerned.
In what might more cynically be viewed as the realm of the innocuous,
the extraneous, and, most often, the quaint, true multiculturalism is
tolerated and encouraged. This realm of cultural alternatives includes
cuisine, folk dance, costume, song, literature, and the like. It also
includes religion, narrowly defined as worship, which in modern society
has been demoted from the earlier place among the cultural universals.
In the final analysis Canadian multiculturalism is political ideology,
even possibly a subtle device to melt the variant immigrants down into
a homogeneous stew.

Conclusion

A deviant minority religious group appears to seek a niche in the
social fabric in one of two ways. It may attempt to isolate members
from the profane non-believing world imposing strict rules of endogamy
and excommunicating those who do not observe the letter of the law.
This mode is best exemplified by the Old Order Amish, the Hutterian
Brethren or, in Jewry, by the Hasidim. The other technique is to pursue an ameliorative role stressing similarities with the prevailing
ideology. The ecumenically oriented churches in Christianity results

from this approach. Canadian Muslims exemplify an ambivalence between the desire to perpetuate the old and a desire to accommodate to the new. Those in the former category must represent a declining group since they are the older in age and the newer or less assimilated immigrants. Elkholy has shown how the more successful Muslim community in the United States appears where there has been some considerable accommodation to American customs (Elkholy, *passim*). Of course the question arises as to what extent this "watered down" Islam is in fact Islam and this indeed is the whole question of the adaptation of Islam to a changing world. In the past Islam was viewed as a total way of life. Presumably there was no difference between secular and sacred. We however may doubt whether this was in fact the case or just a dream perpetuated by religious scholars. In any case transplanted to Canada there is certainly pressure to view Islam as religion as most Christians view Christianity as religion--constituting a specific category in the totality of life without much relationship to the rest.

The balance of evidence supports the thesis that Islam as a religious system inhibits its members from full assimilation to the Canadian context, but this is as it should be since the Canadian context is, after all probably best described as "secular Christian"; it is not the multicultural community taken in any literal sense.

BIBLIOGRAPHY

Abu Laban, Baha, "The Arab Canadian Community" in Elaine C. Hagopian
and Anne Paden (eds.), *The Arab-Americans: Studies in Assimilation*, Willmette, Ill.: Medina University Press, 1969.

Aswad, Barbara (ed.), *Arabic Speaking Communities in American Cities*,
New York: Center for Migration Studies, 1974.

Barclay, Harold B., "A Lebanese Community in Lac La Biche, Alberta" in
Elliott, Jean Leonard, (ed.), *Minority Canadians: Immigrant
Groups*, Scarborough, Ontario: Prentice Hall, 1971.

Barclay, Harold B., "The Lebanese Muslim Family" in Ishwaran, K. (ed.),
The Canadian Family (rev. edition), Toronto, Holt, Rinehart and
Winston, 1976.

Elkholy, Abdo A., *The Arab Moslems in the United States*, New Haven,
Conn.: College and University Press, 1966.

Fathi, Asghar, "Mass Media and a Moslem Immigrant Community in Canada",
Anthropologica, XV, 1973.

Khattab, Abdal Muneim, "The Assimilation of Arab Muslims in Alberta",
M. A. Thesis, University of Alberta, 1969.

Linton, Ralph, *The Study of Man*, New York: Appleton-Century-Croft,
1936.

Lovell, Emily Kalled, "A Survey of the Arab-Muslims in the United
States and Canada", *Muslim World*, LXIII, 1973.

FAITH EXPERIENCES IN TRANSITION AMONG CANADIAN CATHOLICS

I A QUALITATIVE APPROACH

This paper attempts to share some qualitative evidence and provisional conclusions regarding (i) the impact of secularizing and
other societal factors on Canadians in general, and (ii) the impact of
these same factors specifically on four Catholic ethnocultural communities in central Saskatchewan.

The focus of this paper also can be expressed as a question:
"What have been the effects of migration to North America, of life in
Canada, and especially of secularizing influences on the faith experiences and religious expressions of Canadians in general, and of Catholic ethnic groups in particular?"

Some Working Definitions

"Secularization" or "Secularizing Influences":

These expressions are interpreted as referring to all those social
factors which incline citizens to question, modify or abandon their beliefs of faith, religious practices or moral norms based on those beliefs. These secularizing factors are seen to include the consumer
goals and open pluralism of Canadian society today, the presence of
television in virtually every household (thereby bringing to viewers
an endless, unsorted, confusing, conflicting mix of impressions about
the meaning and values of life); the current prevalence of trial unions,
marriage breakdowns, divorce and second marriages; the advent of "the
pill" and other birth-control methods conducive to a "multiple-choice
morality"; the not-so-Quiet Revolution in Quebec; and the renewal initiated in the Catholic church by the Second Vatican Council.

Faith Experiences - How beliefs and moral norms based on these beliefs are seen and experienced. In other words, our perspectives, perceptions, concepts, images and feelings concerning faith and morals;
and the internal meaning and value we give to them.

Religious Expression - How faith and morals are expressed in the
formal practices of worship - private and communal; in daily life - in
the family, at school, and at work; and in public affairs.

Ethnic - Here a more comprehensive word, "ethnoculture", is used
to refer to the distinct origins and ways of life of the various

peoples who make up the Canadian mosaic: Native Peoples, French Canadians, Ukrainian Canadians and the like.

Roman Catholic Ethnic Community - There is no such reality as a
single Roman Catholic ethnic grouping. Instead, in Canada, as in the
universal church, Catholics are a multiracial mosaic of ethnic groups
with distinctive cultural histories and distinctive religious rites.
Examples: French-Canadian Catholics who adhere to the Roman Rite of
Western Spirituality; and Ukrainian-Catholic Canadians who subscribe
to one of the Byzantine Rites of Eastern Spirituality.

Complementary Methods of Research

In this paper very limited reference is made to data gathered by
conventional means. Quantitative head-counting surveys of the Gallup-
Poll variety do provide valuable statistical evidence, of course. They
reveal the statistical skeleton, as it were. But what can bare bones
tell us without the flesh and spirit so essential to any understanding
of the human condition?

In particular research on faith experiences and religious expression calls for something more to complement the statistical approach.
qualitative approach is required--one that attempts to probe under our
skins to the roots of our spiritual beliefs, motives and actions.

As a social journalist primarily interested in attitudinal trends
at the Canadian grassroots, I have been experimenting since 1974 with
one kind of qualitative method. I call it "conversational soundings."
It primarily involves conversational interviews with a broadly representative cross-section of citizens, coast to coast, using several open-
ended questions as discussion starters.

Responses to these conversational soundings are the principal
source of qualitative evidence presented in this paper.

Granted, this method of research raises questions of representa-
tivity and objectivity. Granted also, qualitative data is impossible
to count, difficult to categorize and appraise, and elusive when it
comes to application. All of which difficulties, I would agree, testi-
fies to the humanity of the method. (A detailed account of this method-
ology is given in Instalment III, PROJECT FEEDBACK, Canadian Conference
of Catholic Bishops, 90 Parent Avenue, Ottawa, Ontario K1N 7B1.)

I am persuaded that qualitative soundings of this kind complement
statistical data in a life-giving way. They add flesh and spirit to
the dry statistical bones.

II   CANADIANS IN TRANSITION: AN OVERVIEW

Project Feedback: An Experiment in Social Journalism

In the mid-1970s, when employed by the Canadian Conference of
Catholic Bishops (CCCB) as a social adviser on national and international affairs, I succumbed to a familiar Ottawan disease: bureaucrat-
ic frustration.   I was frustrated by a sense of remoteness from fellow
citizens beyond the untypical environment of the capital.   I was frustrated also by conventional surveys which reported, for example *how*
many Canadians felt organized religion was relevant in their lives, but
which did not shed any light on *why* 50 per cent of respondents felt
this way.

These and other irritations goaded me to test a persisting conviction, based on some years as a media reporter and editor: the conviction that "the brass" always has much to learn from "the grass."
In other words, effective learning and leading are always a two-way process.   As one of the relatively minor brass, I wanted to revisit the
Canadian grassroots so as not to lose contact with "the common touch."
I wished to test my belief that the concerns and hopes identified by
citizens could be of great value to leaders in all fields--*if* leaders
would heed these signals from their constituents.

I hoped to test these assumptions primarily by means of friendly
conversations along the main streets and sideroads of the nation.

Such an experiment in social journalism, called PROJECT FEEDBACK,
was authorized by the CCCB in May 1974.   During the preparatory phase,
I received invaluable assistance from staff colleagues, professional
advisers and fifty local contact-persons across Canada.

The conversational phase began in October 1974.   Over a period of
eight months I asked six basic questions in forty urban and rural communities in all ten provinces.   Conversational interviews with 750
broadly representative citizens and local leaders filled many note
books and nearly 300 cassette tapes.

A free and open exchange was aimed for, whether I was talking with
individuals, couples or small groups.   Almost always, basic trust was
established by means of a brief friendly explanation of what was being
attempted.   It went along these lines: "I'm travelling across Canada
asking fellow citizens at the grassroots how they feel about life today
and in the future.   May I talk with you?"   Above all, this was stressed:
"What I most would like to know is how you, yourself, feel about life.
I would like to quote you without using your name."   Usually that was

assurance enough. Then followed a conversation of forty-five minutes,
more or less, around the six discussion starters. I tried to listen
sensitively--with my heart as well as my head; not in order to judge
or argue but so as to understand the point of view being expressed.
Within the framework of the six generic questions, I made specific queries to help elicit respondents' inner feelings and convictions.

The six starting questions ranged from: "What kind of society
would you like to live in?" to: "What are your views on the meaning
of life?", and: "How do you feel about the future--say ten years from
now?"

Another nine months were required to select, collate and report
some 2,000 typical and insightful comments made by the 750 respondents.
The reports were made in seven instalments, made public from December
1975 through September 1976.

(NOTE: Any instalments still in print are available for
$1.50 each from PROJECT FEEDBACK,© CCCB, 90 Parent Avenue,
Ottawa, Ont. K1N 7B1. FEEDBACK comments cited in this
paper were selected from this copyright material, for which
grateful acknowledgment is made.)

These instalments, plus numerous news stories and media commen-
taries stimulated a continual "feedback on FEEDBACK": Several hundred
letters of opinion, requests and orders for approximately 10,000 copies
of the instalments, and more than 100 invitations to share FEEDBACK experiences with a wide variety of groups: religious to secular, small
to large, local to national. Thus, from March 1976 until now, I have
had opportunities to test FEEDBACK findings and conclusions with at
least 6,000 more Canadians.

So there is much to share in the way of Canadian experiences and
insights about life today and in the future. And how we feel under our
skins is in many respects in sharp contrast to the way we talk and the
way we act in our usual social roles.

Working Hypothesis Based on FEEDBACK Experiences

The FEEDBACK experiment and its sequels are the basis for a two-
point working hypothesis that is central to this presentation:

(i) Individually and in small groups, most Canadians are caught
up, to some degree at least, in a deep-running trend: a trend to blend
elements of the new and the old, of tradition and innovation, into a
more livable balance. This *search for a viable balance* is particularly
evident in daily living, and to a lesser extent in public affairs.

Until twenty to thirty years ago, most Canadians lived mainly by tradition: trying to live in accord with long-established rules and customs, including religious beliefs and prescriptions.

Then in the 1960s and early 1970s cultural change and experimentation became very much the fashion--even, for some, change for its own sake. At times it almost seemed that change was the only remaining constant in life.

This world-wide, American-centered phenomenon of change caused a cultural revolution, Canadian style. This cultural revolution involved new ways of seeing all of life. Perceptions of oneself, neighbors and other people, social institutions, the natural environment, and perceptions of the divine across the human spectrum, such perceptions shifted substantially. As perspectives changed, so did the meaning and value given to the realities and ideals newly perceived. Radical changes in personal behavior and social mores followed. The once prevailing consensus as to what was "real", what to value and how to act gave way to a confused pluralism in a state of flux--one in which all beliefs, values and practices came under question, particularly in interpersonal relationships.

Now, in the latter half of the 1970s, from coast to coast there is a countering trend: an expressed desire to "get back to basics", to sort out values, to identify roots, in the hope of clarifying the confusion caused by rapid, pervasive change.

In this second phase of the ongoing Cultural Revolution, we are seeking a balance between change and continuity in personal and public life, so that we may stay rooted while testing new frontiers. Canadians are searching for a healthy blending that probably differs from region to region, person to person, and from religion to religion.

This ongoing process under our skins brings to mind the familiar parable of the need for both "new wine" and "fresh skins" (*Mark* 2:22). The new wine of evolving outlooks is now fermenting. But what of fresh skins in the form of new social systems and institutions, of "new structures with soul"?

(ii) Unfortunately, and this is the second point of the working hypothesis, *most large institutions in Canadian society lag behind their constituents in the search for a more livable balance of old and new*. Worse, big institutions--Big Governments, Big Business, Big Labor, Big Media, Big Education, and Big Organized Religion--tend to impede individuals and small groups in their quest for a viable blend of tradition and innovation.

"Institutional drag" characterizes many large organizations which,
because they pursue more power, lose their original vision of service
to people, and become instead self-serving mechanisms first of all.

These two points--the widespread personal search for balance and
the hindering effect of "institutional drag"--are conclusively demonstrated, in my view, by FEEDBACK comments, related evidence, and further interviews carried out for this presentation. Here, I will review quickly some of the most pertinent FEEDBACK findings so as to provide a framework for more specific evidence to follow.

Relating to the Ultimate Realities

The process of change that FEEDBACK conversations and other data
reveal is poignantly evident in many citizens unsettled, often anxious
and sometimes anguished stance before the ultimate questions of life
and death. The meanings we ascribe and the values we attribute to the
varied experiences of living, the lasting relationships we seek beyond
deep human friendships: here are the roots of the Canadian search for
a livable balance, for a more nearly fulfilling quality of life.

Here, as in other areas of concern and hope, FEEDBACK respondents
voiced both frustrations and aspirations. Across Canada, in all age,
income, cultural and religious groupings; on the part of both professed believers and professed sceptics, I encountered the same twin
phenomena: spiritual hunger and religious indigestion.

Beyond loneliness, many spoke of an inner emptiness, a hunger for
meanings, values and friendships that last. They craved a lasting food
for the human spirit. While numerous respondents appeared passive,
others searched extensively and intensively in their desire to satisfy
spiritual hunger.

Simultaneously, many of the same respondents and others as well
said they experienced religious indigestion: degrees of hurt, anger,
resentment, bitterness towards big organized religion. In these institutions, their critics complained, they encountered indifference or
hostility instead of fellowship, obscure rituals instead of clear meaning and values, man-made idols instead of the Divine Presence they
sought. Instead of helping them in their quest for spiritual fulfilment, these critics accused institutional religion of hindering their
search, the ultimate crime of spiritual treason!

Other Canadians in large numbers, meanwhile, say that they do find
the spiritual food for which they hunger within the churches and other
religious bodies. Both signs of renewal, especially in smaller groups

and new movements, and signs of institutional retrenchment are abundantly evident in the Christian Churches: a further indication of the widespread search for balance.

Overall, I encountered dozens of Canadians, inside and outside organized religion, who willingly, sometimes eagerly, described their experiences of the divine dimension in life. Known by whatever human name--The Only One, the Great Spirit, Yahweh, Allah, Our Father, Jesus Christ and Holy Spirit--this living, loving Presence is experienced from coast to coast.

Social Indicators of Religious Stance

Samplings of representative FEEDBACK comments provide four social indicators of religious stance:

(1)   In a Canadian milieux of open pluralism now in a state of flux, it is often difficult to distinguish people's *religious origins* by their present-day comments on the ultimate questions.

(2)   It appears equally difficult, oftentimes, to identify their *ethnocultural origins*.

(3)   *Regional - community milieux* are sometimes indicated and sometimes not by such comments.

(4)   However, it appears to be comparatively easy in many, or perhaps most cases to identify the *age groups* by what is said.

Sample FEEDBACK Comments in Age Groups

What about comments of life's meaning and values by *age groups*? Is the age of the speaker usually indicated by the remarks? Consider first some typical comments by Catholic respondents over sixty years of age:

> *A Quebec grandfather had a heart attack while watching a telecast of a hockey game between Montreal and Toronto. He regained consciousness before he died - long enough to ask, "Who won?"*

> *Retired Nova Scotian woman: I'm making a Novena. I don't know if anybody is listening but I'm making it anyway.*

> *Saskatchewan homemaker: God is with us. He said he would never leave us. So why should we worry about the future?*

> *Business executive: One should be simple enough to be able to talk with God--every day. I do.*

Next, comments by Catholics in their middle years, between thirty and sixty:

> *Ontario policeman: The meaning of life is within me. It has nothing to do with anything else.*

Brewery worker: *Before I became involved in the Charis-*
matic Movement, I had an intellectual faith, not a faith
of the heart. Now I'm getting to know the Lord as a
personal savior...

Educator: *Women are put down because of a long tradition*
which puts the blame on Eve and sees the virgin male
priest as the perfect Christian.

Alberta homemaker: *Religion isn't something I put in a*
box marked "Sunday". Everything I do is affected by my
Christian belief.

And finally, viewpoints expressed by Catholic respondents under
30:

Alberta secretary: *I was a Catholic as a kid. We went*
to this small country church every Sunday. The priest
was inhabited by God Himself. You didn't tell him what
you were really thinking because WOW! the Big Thumb might
come down and crush you.

Manitoba teacher: *We don't live by rules now and we don't*
live for laws. We make our own life.

Saskatchewan bank clerk: *I think many people are beginning*
to doubt in God, period. You see the wars, the starvation
and all the other suffering and you wonder, "What in hell
is He doing?"

Young mother, Quebec: *We're not really dropping out of the*
church. We're waiting for the church to catch up to where
we are.

Student in New Brunswick: *We don't have to be scared. Even*
if the church closed, something beautiful will be born.
I'm sure of it.

If these comments had not been grouped by age categories, how many
could have been accurately identified? Most of them, I suggest.

III CATHOLICS IN TRANSITION: FURTHER INDICATIONS

Some Related Evidence

(1) Quebec Catholicism in Transition

One of the most dramatic examples of faith experiences in transition in the industrial world is provided by francophone Catholocism in
Quebec. Here is a notable case study of the secularizing process.

In less than twenty years Quebec Catholics have experienced the
social impact of the Quiet Revolution, initiated by the Lesage government and now expanded by the Levesque regime; rapid industrialization
and urbanization, the arrival of television in virtually every home
(which means French-Canadian programs have to compete with the life-
views and lifestyles promoted by the English-speaking power elite of
North America); new means of contraception, and the cultural religious

upheaval triggered by the renewal initiated at Vatican II. What are
the results?

In less than a generation, French Quebec has been transformed
from a sacral society in which the institutional church was a dominating presence into a secular society in which Catholicism is only one
institutional presence among several, and no longer the most influ-
ential. In less than twenty years, attendance at Sunday Mass declined
drastically, especially in urban working-class areas, reaching a low
of 10% or less in East End Montreal a few years ago. Francophone
couples, meanwhile, changed their views and practices regarding family
size, so that in less than a decade the Quebec birth rate declined
from the second highest to the lowest for any province. At last report, live births among Quebecois was below Z P G (zero Population
Growth).

During this dramatic transition, as a younger bishop points out
with understandable pride, not a single church leader was shot, or
imprisoned or otherwise violently harassed. Quebec Catholocism underwent a visably peaceful, yet radical transition. In the words of one
prelate:

> *"Once everything here was Catholic. Now we have*
> *secularism. Now the real questions have to be*
> *faced by each person: "who am I? Who is God?"*

Among the Quebecois the same basic search for balance continues,
as elsewhere in Canada. Among spiritual leaders, younger Catholic
bishops stand out by their distinctive episcopal style: An articulate
witness of faith, a quiet presence in various public settings, both
social vision and moral courage. Men such as Hubert, Labelle and
Proulx have been tested and tempered by the fires of secularization.
As a new kind of ecclesial leadership, they appear to have left behind
most of the comfortable trappings of the Roman-Empire style of Catholocism in search of a more Gospel-centered Christianity that could be a
lively yeast in the social milieux. In my view, these men and their
collaborators of both sexes are one of the best reasons for not dis-
counting the creative potential of institutional Catholocism in this
country.

(2) <u>Moral Values in Transition: A Saskatchewan Example</u>

Several times annually, the Catholic Centre in Saskatoon sponsors
a Marriage Preparation Course for Catholic and mixed couples. The
Saskatoon Diocese in Central Saskatchewan expects its young couples
entering marriage to enroll for this weekend course in the physical,

psychological, spiritual and financial aspects of Christian Matrimony.
(Half or more of the couples in each course are entering mixed unions,
usually Catholic-Protestant ones.)

When the lectures and discussions end the participants are invited to evaluate the course and answer three value-loaded questions.
There is no doubt what answers would have been expected and almost
always provided by Catholics in generations past. What of today? In
April 1977 some 220 young adults responded and in June another 180 answered the three questions. The results are a further indication of
how most young adults, a majority of them Catholic in this instance,
appraise life's meanings and values:

> *Q - Do you believe marriage to be a commitment*
> *until death?*
>
> *90 percent answered "yes" in both April and*
> *June, indicating that the traditional ideal*
> *of marriage for life remains popular. (One*
> *observer voiced this caution: "Even though*
> *sincere, most of that 90 percent probably*
> *have the divorce option in the back of their*
> *minds nowadays.")*
>
> *Q - Do you feel that the desire to have a child*
> *is an essential part of married love?*
>
> *55 percent answered "yes" in April and June.*
> *30 to 33 percent said "no".*
>
> *Q - Do you believe that a couple should wait*
> *until after their wedding before engaging in*
> *sexual intercourse?*
>
> *"No" said 60-65 percent at the two courses.*
> *20 percent were "not sure". Only 11-13 per-*
> *cent said "yes", they thought they should wait.*

Together, the three majority answers - 90 percent "yes" to a lifetime marriage, a two-thirds "yes" to premarital sex, and a less prevalent 55 percent "yes" to child-bearing--seem to represent a significant
blending of traditional Catholic standards and modern secular mores.
Unmistakably, the majority answers are those of the generation under
thirty.

(3) Faith Experiences in Four Ethnocultural Catholic Communities
     of Central Saskatchewan, Summer, 1977: An Initial Probe

The foregoing evidence whetted my appetite for further data. With
this paper primarily in mind, I made conversational soundings in the
familiar territory of central Saskatchewan in July 1977.

By way of an initial and limited probe, I decided to interview a
minimum number of knowledgeable Catholics belonging to different ethnocultural groups and living within a 150-mile radius of Saskatoon.

Because of its size and complexity, I passed over the Irish/Scottish Catholic sub-culture in which I was raised as the child of mixed Catholic-Methodist marriage. Instead, I sought out several members of four smaller ethnic groups: from among Ukrainian Canadians, who make up nine percent of the Saskatchewan population; French Canadians, who constitute six percent; German Canadians of Russo and Deutsche origins, who are nine percent; and Polish Canadians, who make up three percent of the province's multicultural mosaic.

Saskatoon counts two large Ukrainian Catholic parishes belonging to the Byzantine Rite. I invited a few members to describe their faith experiences as rural children and now as urban adults. Within thirty-five miles of Saskatoon there are three bilingual, still primarily francophone churches at Vonda, St. Denis and Prud' homme. I sought out insights about religious and ethnocultural expression in this urban-rural milieu. Fifty miles further east is Muenster, site of St. Peter's Abby, the spiritual centre of the Benedictine clergy first settled by German-American Catholics in the early 1900s. I interviewed a few members in this rural-urban setting. Then I drove to Kuroki, another seventy-five miles east, where I joined 200 mostly Polish-Catholic couples and children for a Family Day Rally. This provided some first hand impressions of life in a primarily rural milieu that still contains some reminders of a cultural enclave.

In the conversational interviews and at the Rally I talked with Catholics who belong to the transitional generation between thirty and sixty years of age, including married couples, pastors, writers and teachers. I chose members of the middle generation for this limited probe because they remember the traditional ways even as they experience and adapt to the new.

These informal conversations focussed on the central question of how societal factors have affected faith experiences and religious expressions in the respondents' ethnocultural milieux. As we talked, I asked several related questions. Respondents shared their experiences and insights frankly and with feeling. Here are some selected comments, first impressions and provisional conclusions:

(1)   The Religious Life

Ukrainian Canadian Catholics

The religious faith we grew up with was pretty much as it was brought over from the Ukraine and white Russia.

I remember the family driving nearly ten miles by wagon or cutter to church for long religious ceremonies. Especially at Christmas and Easter, which were three-day celebrations...The Divine Liturgy was very long. You were never sure when it would begin or end. It was conducted in old Slavnic which we didn't understand. I remember being restless. I was never really sure what the Mass was.

The adults stood in church, men on the right, women on the left. In the summertime some of the men would go outside to smoke and talk together.

Great reverence was shown to the clergy, who were educated. The whole household prepared before the priest came to stay overnight. Children were admonished to be on their best behavior.

My parents looked on the nearest Roman Catholic Church as "the Polish church." Poles were seen as enemies of the Ukrainian church, for historical reasons.

Now the Ukrainian church has become less nationalistic. Even the cathedral church does not maintain a complete national identity, not even in language.

French Canadian Catholics

Twenty-five to thirty years ago 90 to 95 percent were church-goers. Those who didn't go were singled out. There were many opportunities to practice: feast days, fast days, Holy Week, forty hours, Missions, May and October as the months of Mary, frequent confession and less frequent communion.

Now, about 60 percent are regular practicioners, while 15-20 percent observe periodically. There are far fewer occasions for public worship: Sunday Mass and not much else.

Lenten practices symbolize the way it used to be: daily Mass, real fasting, the Way of the Cross. All building up to Holy Week and Easter. Now the symbol might be a Parish Council meeting or a workshop on adult religious education. Before lay people went to church and didn't speak up. Now they go to meetings and speak out.

German Canadian Catholics

Every morning, winter and summer, we kids walked three miles to eight o'clock Mass, sent off by our Mother. After Mass came catechism classes. We memorized the required answers, which were gibberish to us.

The parish priest was a scary figure. Very formal, and he had no time for children. I recall all that as an unhuman experience. Fear predominated...Except for very loving grandparents, who were pious. If they could suffer through it, so could we kids.

Back then 95 percent observed Sunday. People who didn't were considered mavericks. Now Sunday observance would be around 75 percent. Quite a few teenagers and young adults don't go regularly.

We used to depend totally on religious leaders for all the answers. Now the leaders waffle on the difficult

*moral questions. There is less show of respect for
clergy and sisters.*

Polish Canadian Catholics

*At the Kuroki Deanery Rally, careful respect was paid
to the clergy, but lay leaders directed the day's program. Except for two brief intervals of prayer, visiting and local clergy maintained a low profile. The
concluding Eucharist, conducted wholly in English, was
as updated as the average Roman Liturgy in a large city.
The sermon by Archbishop Halpin of Regina stressed lay
responsibilities.*

The foregoing comments and observance indicate that attitudes towards worship and the clergy, and formal religious practices, have all
changed substantially in the four communities.

(2) Family and Work Life

Ukrainian Canadian Catholics

*Each year we used to celebrate about two dozen feast days--
St. Stephen's, St. Basil's and so on. No farm work was
done on those days - no gardening, no chicken-plucking.
Everything stopped, even harvesting, for the high holy
days. I miss those feasts now.*

*Our parents wanted us to get a university education. In
the rural areas teaching was a highly respected profes-
sion. So we were urged to go to teachers' college or
business college. Ours was the first generation to become urbanized.*

French Canadian Catholics

*Locally, there is no pressure to be other than French and
Catholic. The social pressures come from outside - especially from TV which brings a mixture of values into our
homes.*

German Canadian Catholics

*We used to have long family prayers, on our knees, led by
my father. The Rosary was recited in German.*

*These days even some of the older married couples are
breaking up.*

Polish Canadian Catholics

*Family ties appear strong in the Kuroki district. More
than 200 men, women and children attended the July Rally
on a sunny working day. Three generations were present:
some grandparents, many parents, and numerous children
ranging from babies to teenagers. This kind of three-
generation solidarity is not ordinarily seen outside of
closely-knit rural communities or urban ethnic districts.*

*At first glance local family life seemed idyllic. Later
in the day, quite a few parents, especially mothers, con-
fided their worries about sons' and daughters' dating
practices and marital problems.*

Again, similar patterns of change are described in the four communities.

(3) ## Citizenship

Ukrainian Canadian Catholics

*I grew up in a rural cultural ghetto. When I started high
school in town I acquired a desire to become part of the
larger community.*

*Before there was more emphasis on Christian home life.
Now there is more on our social obligations as Christians.*

French Canadian Catholics

*This community of Catholics is more cultural than Chris-
tian in its living. What comes across is that these are
white, middle-class North Americans. The faith dimension
does not single us out. And yet, paradoxically, we still
derive some identity and security from the Catholic Way.*

*There's a growing scepticism about all values and insti-
tutions. This affects our religious stance. We're suffering from confusion over values to live by. Maternal well-
being is a soporific that tends to dull our deeper concerns.*

German Canadian Catholics

*When I was growing up the private, personal morality among
adults was probably high, whether out of social habit or
conviction I don't know.*

*I cannot recall much evidence of social concern. For
awhile it was really taboo to look at the CCF party (fore-
runner to the NDP) even though this area elected the first
Catholic MLA belonging to the new party.*

*According to the local Mounties, this is still an unusually
law-abiding area, except for the drinking problem.*

Polish Canadian Catholics

*Hard work and material success appear to be major civic
virtues among Polish Catholics--just as they are among
their Catholic neighbors to the west.*

*During a one-day visit I saw several indications that out-
side factors were affecting this once rather immune enclave.
An older priest spoke of his wish for closer co-operation
between Polish Catholics and their Ukrainian Catholic and
Orthodox neighbors, even though they had been enemies in
the past. A retired farmer wished that Protestant neighbors had been invited to the Family Day Rally, saying:
"It's time we were all Christians now." During the after-
noon entertainment a local singer led the rally in rousing
Protestant hymns; many appeared to know the lyrics. And
all three generations seemed to enjoy a modern drama about
religions in Saskatchewan, "Prairie Psalms", which was performed by talented young members of the Twenty-Fifth Street
Players from Saskatoon. These were more of the evident signs
of the Kuroki area's openness to other ways of seeing life
and living it.*

Ethnocultural and religious accommodations are evident in virtually every comment and observation. And what of language - that
traditional touchstone of cultural identity?

(4) Language

Ukrainian Canadian Catholics

*Once the Divine Liturgy was only celebrated in old Slav-
onic. In our parish now two of the Sunday Masses are in
English and one in Ukrainian. Even at the Cathedral two
of the Masses are in English. All according to the Byzantine Rite, of course.*

*The fact that many Ukrainians married Latin Rite Catholics
and Protestants was an important factor in these language
changes.*

*Today a majority of young Ukrainian adults only know Eng-
lish. If they are to keep in touch with their Ukrainian
roots, it has to be in English. This means they cannot
appreciate some aspects of their heritage when they don't
know Ukrainian, but overall, I would say our children are
very interested in learning about their Ukrainian traditions in English, and are richer for it.*

French Canadian Catholics

*Once this small triangle of territory was the provincial
centre of French cultural aspirations. Francophones still
make up three quarters of the parishioners. Perhaps half
of them still have the energy to maintain their cultural
identity, their language. With the language they can live
with a French-Canadian soul - with a special sense of belonging both to Canada and to Quebec. Without the language, all else is common.*

*Effectively, there is very little French in our schools
after grade six. And we have to teach catechism in
English to be fully understood.*

*The parish church is not promoting francophone culture
but it does respect the will to survive culturally, without becoming militant about it.*

*Can we be genuinely multicultural without being multi-
lingual? Beyond cooking our ethnic meal or doing a
cultural dance? Probably a second or third level of
cultural identity is possible, and basically healthy.*

Polish Canadian Catholics

*Polish expressions used in friendly conversations were
overheard only a few times. The Rally program, like the
Mass, was conducted solely in English.*

Among the four ethnocultural groups visited, only the francophones
still struggle to maintain their mother tongue. And even the francophones do so with what appears to be diminishing confidence and vigor.

(5) Attitudes of Older and Younger Generations

Ukrainian Canadian Catholics

Our parents to this day carry on the traditions we grew up with.

Our oldest daughter and her husband flew home to have their first child baptized in our parish church.

My son-in-law became a Ukrainian-Rite Catholic but he wouldn't grovel. He wouldn't put up with what our generation did when converting - insulting questions, conditional baptism and all the rest.

French Canadian Catholics

The older generation is quiet, resigned, basically secure. They have enough basic faith in God to believe that He will have His way.

A young couple who no longer are regular church-goers had their child baptized recently. The grandmother was the prime mover. It's not hard to call people back to their family roots. It's the only place where such a ritual still makes sense. Back in the family you don't have to try to reconcile it with secularized living.

Among young people there is still some thirst for searching, but not much energy for it. The search is usually postponed because the main social demand is to "make it" financially.

German Canadian Catholics

Most old people seem to go along with the changes. Perhaps they are conditioned by TV.

Young people are less devout now but they ask more questions and are more inclined to think things through.

Youth are strongly secularized. Religious observances don't mean much. Most take their values from TV, from friends. They are really in love with good jobs, money, cars and freedom.

When my grade twelve class in Ethics discussed what Christianity is really all about, they say, "Now that we know what it is, we're not afraid of it."

Polish Canadian Catholics

At Kuroki we invited teenagers to join parents and grandparents in the group discussions. They did so willingly. Some used this opportunity to argue vigorously with their elders about issues of sexual morality. Only one parent was seen to become visibly angry.

As in previous evidence, the views of the young that emerged in four Saskatchewan communities are in sharp contrast to those of their seniors on virtually every major count.

(6) Quality of Faith Then and Now

Ukrainian Canadian Catholics

For those who believe faith is as strong, if not stronger than before. There's more appreciation now as to what the Eucharist is about. Probably there's not yet a greater appreciation of the Gospel. Still there's some thrust in the direction of Christian living in all aspects of life.

French Canadian Catholics

The quality of relating to God may be about the same, although the cultural environment is much less supportive than it was. The sense of God has receded. There are fewer reminders in society of His Presence. But the thirst is not quenched.

The institutional church does not have the control over people that it had twenty years ago. People have taken their distance - more in scepticism than because of hostility.

German Canadian Catholics

Church-going was once the thing to do. Sunday was sacred. For us it was an oasis in the week, a welcome day off from six days of hard work. The whole family enjoyed the day. Is there a chance of keeping that Sunday tradition alive?

Back then any expression of religious belief was formal, from the book. Now people are ready to speak spontaneously of their religious views.

Polish Canadian Catholics

The expressions of faith, so far as could be gauged from a one-day visit, seemed sincere. As visitors from an urban environment we wondered to ourselves how well this still socially-supported faith would fare in a less friendly milieux.

These qualitative readings, limited and provisional, are rather mixed. And what of the future - in terms of religious faith and ethnocultural expressions of that faith?

(7) Prospects?

Ukrainian Canadian Catholics

The adaptability of our parish, and the increasing vocations among Ukrainian Redemptorists are some reasons to feel hopeful about the future.

French Canadian Catholics

The best thing to do today is to work on the foundations and witness to them: to a living, loving God, that Jesus is real, that life ultimately makes sense, that the Gospel is the most life-giving of all stories.

We have forty trained catechists working with six to eight teenagers each. Each group is trying to react in a Christian way to an overwhelming environment.

In terms of faith, the trend is to a purer expression: less of a Christendom approach, more of leaven in society. In terms of cultural, francophone expression will decrease still more. The assimilating trend will continue.

For myself, I have unqualified hope because I trust in Him. He will make His Way known whatever we do.

German Canadian Catholics

Young families are coming along. Their small children seem so alive and open. I'd put the future in their hands very eagerly.

It will be more difficult to keep Sunday and marriage as vital Christian witnesses. If I'm optimistic about the future, it's more because of some of the secular trends. Plus the hope that we may find new ways of being church.

Polish Canadian Catholics

I would predict that a visitor to Kuroki Deanery ten years hence will find Catholic belief and practice still prevalent - at least within the confines of the parish church and the average family circle.

Personally, after these four samplings I continue to hope--even though now more inclined to doubt--that ten to twenty years from now proportionately more Christians, Protestants and Catholics, will be committed to the radical version and ethic of the Scriptures: those testimonies which continually challenge secular views, values and practices in personal living and in public affairs.

IV SUMMING UP

The principal conclusion to be drawn from this qualitative evidence seems to me very clear: sooner or later, the dominant culture--its social perceptions, language, priority values and social mores--virtually absorbs ethnic subcultures. This trend is to be expected particularly in an open, pluralist milieux; Television alone will bring the dominant culture's message into every home every day.

The dominating majority culture, of course, is the primarily American continental culture of which Canada, and especially English-speaking Canada, is an integral part. Whether or not we approve is hardly the point. This dominating culture is power-revering, profit-making, consumer-oriented, religiously "neutral" and thoroughly secular. In this technocratic culture, to cite George F. Will in *Newsweek*, (August 8, 1977), "Modern man (is) proudly sovereign beneath a blank heaven."

A Proposal for "Images" Research

The initial evidence and conclusions presented here point to the need for more research into the correlations between religious faith, ethnocultures and secularizing factors in Canadian society. What, first of all, is happening to perceptions and images of the divine among Canadians?

> *The God question is first. What happens to the institutional church is a secondary question.*

This comment by a FEEDBACK respondent is a reminder that however prevalent religious indigestion may be, a spiritual hunger for some lasting meaning and value in life remains. Another respondent suggests that renewed interest in the occult, exorcist-style movies and widespread fascination with UFOs and "Abominable Snowmen" are further signs of this human craving for mystery. And I'm inclined to agree with a friend who believes that some people become alcoholics because they are "frustrated mystics."

There is considerable evidence indicating that perceptions of the divine are shifting markedly for many today. The once prevalent image of God as a rather vengeful old man up there in the sky is finally giving way (thank God!) to a deepening sense of Presence in here - in oneself. Some 40,000 readers of *Psychology Today*, many of them without religious affiliation, reported this sense of "God in the gut" in responding to that magazine's religious survey. (See *Psychology Today*, November 1974). During FEEDBACK interviews, many respondents stressed this sense of immanence more than they did an awareness of transcendence. These comments by a man and woman indicate the trend:

> <u>Man:</u> *It's a question of God with me. I've discarded the old images. Now I see God as a pervading intelligence in nature, of which I am a part. I'm directed from within. For what purpose I do not know.*

> <u>Woman:</u> *I know God exists but I really couldn't say how exactly. You feel Him. You know He's there. Or else what's the purpose of life?*
> *As a child I thought He was floating up there somewhere. This used to be very scary to me, like a club over my head.*
> *Then I came down to earth. Now it's an inside feeling. I can even imagine Him chuckling. But sometimes I don't understand Him. If He is that powerful, why all the suffering and all the wars? Why does He let us get away with it?...*

Profound implications for daily living by this man and woman follow from their particular images of the divine. Likewise for the rest of us, whatever our perceptions may be. Yet we know comparatively little about one another's "effective images" of God, humanity, society and church. Until more is known, a creative catechesis will largely elude spiritual leaders in communicating their teachings on faith and morals. This is the position of Reverend Marcel Gervais, director of Divine Word, a centre for Scriptural Studies in London, Ontario.

The Gervais thesis is further evidence of the need for more research into shifting perceptions and attitudes towards the ultimate realities of life. Several methods should be used: quantative surveys which yield statistical data, and qualitative soundings which provide further insights into what people believe and why. Indeed, the qualitative and quantitative methods could be tested in some creative blending. When I suggested this to a senior representative of Gallup, the response was positive. Gallup spokesman offered to collaborate in devising and testing a pilot survey using both quantifiable questions of the "Yes-No-Don't Know" variety, and qualitative queries as to *why* respondents say "Yes", "No" and "Don't Know." This is one of the most promising research opportunities awaiting attention.

Were "image" research carried out, the findings--if taken seriously--would surely assist spiritual leaders to narrow the present credibility gap between believers in transition and religious institutions which lag behind them.

Institutional leaders need all the help they can muster. FEEDBACK responses and related evidence indicate that while numerous Canadians expect spiritual experiences will become increasingly important in their lives, many predict that religion be less important to them, at least in present forms.

For all believers, the signs and portents are mixed. In the secular climate now prevalent across Canada, some of us feel at one with the religious sister in Quebec who said:

> *I feel we have to accept this situation of starting off in the dark, without being in the light. We have to begin again with total faith like Abraham and Sarah.*

RELIGION, ETHNICITY AND PUBLIC POLICY

The chief objective of this conference is "to examine the effect that living in Canada has had upon the religious practice of various ethnic groups." My task is to discuss the changing role of "mainline" Anglo-Saxon Protestant groups. This involves a rather sharp shift in perspective. The groups dealt with by the other speakers are minorities in Canada. Anglo-Saxon Protestantism, on the other hand, refers to the religion and ethnicity of the major power holders during the formative period in the development of Canadian society.

This shift in focus from minority to majority can be pictured in terms of the Gestalt figure-ground image. Other speakers have dealt with colourful figures against a grey WASP background. However, if the argument I intend to develop in this paper is sound, this shift from figure to ground will be temporary. The large Protestant denominations, such as the United, Anglican and Presbyterian, will reappear as minority figures against the new background of a post-Christendom society. My aim in this paper is to explore this shift from majority to minority status, and to reflect upon its meaning for the religious practice of the mainline Anglo-Saxon Protestant groups in modern Canada.

Changes in the role and self-understanding of the large Protestant denominations can be discussed in relation to different theories about the assimilation of non-Anglo-Saxons into Canadian society. As Howard Palmer points out, the three theories which have dominated discussions of immigrant or minority-group adjustment are: 1. Anglo-conformity; 2. the melting pot; and, 3. the mosaic or multiculturalism.[1]

It is with great caution that I imply that there has been a development from Anglo-conformity and melting pot theories to a commitment to cultural pluralism. On the one hand, most minorities continue to find conformity to Anglo-Saxon ways the price required to become integrated into Canadian society. On the other hand, the assumption that Canada is a mosaic goes a long way back in our history. Such a development does, however, appear to characterize crucial shifts in the self-understanding of the mainline Anglo-Saxon Protestant churches. It is that development that primarily concerns me in this paper.

I

The Anglo-conformity theory of immigrant adjustment is rooted in
the Conquest, the influence of United Empire Loyalists, and in Lord
Durham's famous Report. In his proclamation of October 9, 1838, Lord
Durham declared:

> My aim was to elevate the Province of Lower Canada
> to a thoroughly British character. I hoped to con-
> fer on an united people a more extensive enjoyment
> of free and responsible government, and to merge
> the petty jealousies of a small community, and the
> odious animosities of origin, in the higher feelings
> of a nobler and more comprehensive nationality.[2]

The interesting question for the student of religion, of course,
is how this proposed identity for British North America was sacralized
or legitimated. As Hans Mol points out, religion can be defined as
"the *sacralization of identity*". Sacralization refers, according to
Mol, "to the process by means of which on the level of symbol-systems
certain patterns acquire the same taken-for-granted, stable, eternal
quality which on the level of instinctive behaviour was acquired by the
consolidation and stabilization of new genetic materials." Sacralization "is the inevitable process that safeguards identity when it is endangered by the disadvantages of the infinite adaptability of symbol-
systems." It "protects identity, a system of meaning, or a definition
of reality, and modifies, obstructs, or (if necessary) legitimates
change."[3]

For the early stages of British settlement the dominant identity
was sacralized by the Church of England. The colonial administrators
assumed that the Church of England should be the legally established
church in the colonies as it was in England. The successful war of
independence in the United States underlined the importance of Church
establishment. The Tories defended it because it was a God-given, pro-
vidential institution. For the Whigs it was a useful device for incul-
cating loyalty to British institutions and the British connection. As
J. L. H. Henderson says in his article, "The Abominable Incubus: The
Church as by Law Established":

> The new government needed support, needed the sanctions
> of religion, needed intelligent and persistent advocacy
> among the people, needed it desperately among the French
> and therefore worked through Roman Catholic bishops and
> clergy, needed it among the English speaking and was
> more or less prepared to pay the price. Grenville and
> Pitt saw it as the error of their predecessors that in
> the general policy of assimilating the American colonies
> to the British constitution, the church had been

neglected. The church also needed the support of
government. How else could these raw settlements
be given the sacraments and the solace of religion,
let alone the buildings?[4]

The universe did not unfold the way the Church of England supporters had hoped it would. The Quebec Act of 1774 had entrenched the
rights of the Roman Catholic Church in Lower Canada. The rapid expansion and growing respectability of the Methodists in the Maritimes and
Upper Canada prompted them to modify their voluntaristic, sectarian origins. They joined the struggle in Upper Canada for a share of the
Clergy Reserves, and for public support for their Indian missions and
denominational college. By the 1850s the division of the Clergy Reserves, the secularization of the endowment for a university, and the
creation of a common, non-sectarian school system, marked the end of an
era. An era characterized by formal church establishment and dissent-
ing or non-conformist sects and minority churches. Formal disestablish-
ment did not, however, produce a religiously neutral state. Nor did it
produce equality among religious groups. The mainline Protestant churches assumed and were granted a superior role in the promotion of what
Robert Handy has called, "voluntary Christendom."[5]

The unifying image underlying this Protestant nation-building mission was the vision of Canada as "His Dominion." As Keith Clifford
points out:

> This Canadian version of the Kingdom of God had sig-
> nificant nationalistic and millenial overtones, and
> sufficient symbolic power to provide the basis for
> the formation of a broad Protestant consensus and
> coalition. Not only the major Protestant denomina-
> tions but also a host of Protestant-oriented organi-
> zations such as temperance societies, missionary
> societies, Bible societies, the Lord's Day Alliance,
> the YMCA's and YWCA's utilized this vision as a frame-
> work for defining their task within the nation, for
> shaping their conceptions of the ideal society, and
> for determining those elements which posed a threat
> to the realization of their purposes.[6]

A major threat to this vision was the massive immigration of non-
Anglo-Saxons to Canada in the late nineteenth and early twentieth centuries. The dominant Protestant response to this threat was to become
active agents of assimilation. W. B. Creighton, editor of the United
Church's paper, *The New Outlook*, reflected a perceptive awareness that,
in relation to the task of assimilating non-Anglo-Saxons, the church
had an important sacralizing role. In an editorial in 1925 he said:

> Large sections of our Dominion are being filled with
> a polyglot people. ...The problem which confronts
> our statesmen and all who have at heart the true

> welfare of our nation in the future is how to fuse
> these diverse elements in our population so as to
> form one great and homogeneous community committed
> to the highest ideals of what is best in our modern
> Christian civilization. The school has a great func-
> tion to perform in this direction.
> ...But neither the school nor the workshop, nor the
> mart, go down to the deepest springs of life. Our
> religious feelings and interests reach down to what
> is deepest in our common manhood, and it is on this
> sacred ground that we are drawn most closely and
> sympathetically together.

According to Creighton, the church was "the country's real 'melting pot' because while an 'alien may speak our language, wear our clothes and buy our wares', he does not really become a Canadian until 'his moral standards and ideals become our standards and ideals'."[7]

Creighton used the language of melting pot but there is little question that he meant Anglo-Saxon Protestant standards and ideals. Like most liberal Protestants between the 1850s and the 1950s, he "saw the church as the institution responsible for the maintenance and trans- mission of the nation's most sacred ideals and values."[8] By mid-cen- tury, however, this Protestant consensus had collapsed. The image of Canada as "His Dominion" no longer reflected either Canadian reality or the self-understanding of the mainline Protestant churches. The post- war years seemed to be a time of pragmatic problem-solving, rather than nation-building in accordance with a dominant image or a grand scheme for Canada's future. It is as a negative image characterizing the domi- nant trends in Canadian society, as opposed to an ideal to be pursued, that the melting pot captures the mood of the post-war period.

                                   II

I realize that the melting pot is normally associated with the United States.[9] It never became an ideal to be pursued in Canada as it was south of the border. Rather, melting pot assumptions about non- Anglo-Saxon assimilation were the product of environmentalist and func- tionalist modes of thought which treated religion and ethnicity as pri- vate matters.[10] This tendency is well illustrated in Carl Dawson's 1936 study of the assimilation of Doukhobors, Mennonites, Mormons, Ger- man Catholics and French Canadians on the prairies.[11]

For example in his analysis of the assimilation of the German- Catholics, Dawson acknowledged the importance of where the railroad was located on the fate of the church-centred, German-Catholic communities. He concluded, however, that the replacement of these communities by the

new commercial towns located along the railway was the result of "natural" forces working in the environment. In his words:

> All of these communities have been subject to the
> play of natural forces which operated to break
> down the barriers which separated the homogeneous
> groups from their neighbours. ...it seems clear
> from the evidence analysed that the unplanned play
> of external forces in the long run tends to elimi-
> nate much, perhaps all, of the distinctiveness of
> separatist colonies.

According to Dawson, this process could be aided by well-administered
policies, but it should not be hurried by consciously pursuing anglicization or assimilation as goals. He concluded:

> Schools and other governmental regulations, when
> wisely administered, facilitate enormously the
> apparently inevitable assimilation of these eth-
> nic minorities. Some of those who have attempted
> to hasten this assimilation by ill-chosen means,
> have unwittingly retarded it by arousing the self-
> consciousness and recalling the receding solidarity
> of these colonies. Assimilation may be facilitated
> by extending types of social organization to these
> ethnic communities if administrators learn how to
> work with the inevitable tide rather than against
> it.[12]

Dawson's conclusions about assimilation must be seen in relation to
his assumptions about secularization. In his view:

> Assimilation to the more secular world surrounding
> and invading these colonies calls for a considera-
> tion of the subsidiary processes of *secularization*.
> Secular values, as distinct from sacred, are cal-
> culable, utilitarian and mundane. They are largely
> divested of emotion and sentiment, and involve atti-
> tudes which reflect, in a measure, the critical de-
> tachment of science.[13]

By assuming that the society into which the minority groups were
being assimilated based its public policies on "calculable, utilitarian
and mundane" values, which were "largely divested of emotion and senti-
ment," Dawson could ignore the continuing role of the religious senti-
ments and ethnic loyalties presupposed by the dominant social group.
He could overlook the fact that Ontario Protestant entrepreneurs, bureaucrats and politicians could adopt a detached view of the fate of the
German-Catholic, church-centred communities because their own identity
was not threatened.

I find Dawson's study interesting because the same basic attitude
on the part of the dominant English-speaking society towards unassimi-
lated fragments still exists. One need think only of the way the
English-speaking air traffic controllers and pilots submerged the language issue under their rhetoric about "safety in the air," and English

as the universal language of the airways. In a similar fashion, southern Canadians so take for granted the legitimacy or inevitability of
the exploitation of frontier oil and gas that the extent to which different ways of life are in conflict in the northern pipeline debate is
obscured if not denied. What is perhaps changing, however, is the nature of the dominant identity and the way it is sacralized.

A countervailing tradition within the social sciences is emerging
which challenges the adequacy of the conventional social scientific
assumptions about secularization and modernization. Scholars such as
Milton Yinger, Thomas Luckmann, Andrew Greeley, Hans Mol and Gregory
Baum, to name just a few whose works have influenced my own approach to
the study of religion, suggest that we must learn to see the modern
period as a time of religious change rather than religious decline.[14]
It is, in their view, a category mistake to equate the declining influence of a particular religious tradition with the disappearance of religion. It is also a mistake to confuse the changing organizational
form of a particular religious tradition with the disappearance of that
tradition. Thus, two questions, which have been neglected even by soci-
ologists of religion, are: What is the continuing role of Anglo-Saxon
Protestantism in the legitimation or sacralization of the dominant
Canadian identity? And, if the influence of traditional church religion
has declined, what has taken its place as the sacralizing agency for
the identity of modern society?

In his recent overview of mainline Protestantism in Canada and the
United States, Harold Fallding stresses the continuing influence of
Protestantism on our so-called secular society. He maintains that:
"the dynamism of modern culture is largely Protestantism's own creation,
and Protestantism has then continually to minister to people at the
avant garde positions into which it has propelled them."[15] From this
point of view, the basic role of the Protestant churches has not
changed. They continue to sacralize the dominant ethos, even though
they appear to focus primarily on the needs of individuals for salvation
and/or peace of mind.

Another possibility, however, is that the identity of the dominant
social group in Canada depends only in a residual way on the sacralizing
function of Protestantism. Perhaps the industrial-technological system
itself has evolved its own mechanisms of sacralization which perform the
legitimating functions for modern society that Protestantism performed
during earlier stages of development.

It is in relation to this possibility that it is interesting to
examine the shifting emphasis within Protestantism between sacralizing
Canada's existing dominant identity and legitimating challenges to that
identity. My starting point for exploring this question is the recent
wave of enthusiasm for multiculturalism or cultural pluralism. My basic point will be that not only must we question what it means to say
that Canada is a secular society, we must also ask to what extent it is
pluralistic.

III

Palmer suggests that multiculturalism presupposes "the preservation of some aspects of immigrant culture and communal life within the
context of Canadian citizenship and political and economic integration
into Canadian society."[16] But what are the characteristics associated
with Canadian citizenship? One of my American students once told me
that he was given a job by an employer who expressed relief that finally
a Canadian had applied for the job! What is meant by political and
economic integration into Canadian society? The 1965 Canadian Institute for Cultural Research study of name changing reports that one man
changed his name because "It is easier for my children in school to
have an Anglo-Saxon name."[17] Other respondents were reluctant to change
their names because they had feelings of loyalty and pride regarding
their ethnic origins. However, "practicality and reality" won, and they
changed their names in the interests of their careers. What is the
Canadian "reality" that shapes the way we respond in our public roles?
How is it related to the Federal Government's multiculturalism policy,
and to the religious practice of the mainline Protestant churches?

When Prime Minister Trudeau introduced the federal multiculturalism
policy to the House of Commons on October 8, 1971, he said: "Although
there are two official languages, there is no official culture, nor does
any ethnic group take precedence over any other. No citizen or group of
citizens is other than Canadian, and all should be treated fairly." To
implement the policy the government promised "to assist all Canadian
cultural groups--to continue to grow and contribute to Canada;" "to
overcome the cultural barriers to full participation in Canadian society;" to promote "interchanges--in the interest of national unity;" and
"to assist immigrants to acquire at least one of Canada's official languages in order to become full participants in Canadian society." He concluded by emphasizing that it was "the view of the government that a

policy of multiculturalism within a bilingual framework is basically
the conscious support of individual freedom of choice."[18]

It is important to ask, however, whether the Federal Government's
multiculturalism policy is merely a sophisticated modern version of
Lord Durham's desire to embrace all non-Anglo-Saxon groups in "a nobler
and more comprehensive nationality" which remains essentially Anglo-
Saxon? Perhaps it reflects careful attention to Dawson's advice that:
"Assimilation may be facilitated by extending types of social organization to these ethnic communities if administrators learn how to work
with the inevitable tide rather than against it?"

I am prepared to grant that the Federal Government's emphasis on
multiculturalism is sincere, and not a mere smoke screen to hide the
old Anglo-conformity or melting pot models of immigrant adjustment.
What I do see happening, however, is that the cultural differences
which are tolerated, consumed, and perhaps even respected, involve
private matters. They deal with instruction in a second language, and
modes of dress, recreation and weekend behaviour. Folk-dances, ethnic
restaurants, and diverse forms of religious worship enhance the freedom of choice of participants and consumers alike. They do not, however, challenge our dominant attitudes towards resource development,
relations between rich and poor, and what it means to be a success in
modern Canada. They might even provide escapes which help us to adjust
to the conformity required in our jobs and other public roles.

It seems to me, therefore, that the Federal Government's multiculturalism policy has received wide acceptance by the media and other
opinion-molding elites because it does not go beyond the reigning consensus which undergirds Canada's identity as an industrial society.

Until recently the mainline Protestant churches have been participants in the liberal, mixed economy, melting pot consensus which was
so characteristic of the 1950s but which still survives. The Federal
Government's multiculturalism policy, and the churches shift in emphasis
from anglicizing and Christianizing non-Anglo-Saxons and non-Christians
are well within the broad limits of this consensus. For example in
Ontario the Conservative government received widespread support when it
blocked the attempt of the North York Board of Education to extend public aid to a Jewish school. The government interpreted "freedom of
choice" (to be excused from religious instruction) as applying to individuals within each school. The Jewish community regarded "freedom of
choice" as the freedom to choose between schools. The Jewish parents
who want to have their children educated in a Jewish ethos must pay

extra for this "private" schooling. That is, they must adjust to the
Canadian consensus based on an "individualistic" concept of freedom of
choice.

The relationship between freedom of the individual and freedom for
one's group depends, however, upon whether one is part of the majority
or a member of a minority. The majority can simply take its collective
identity for granted, and, thus appear to be very individualistic.
This tendency for mainline Protestants to be insensitive to the rights
of minorities as distinctive ethnic or religious groups was also illustrated in the recent debate in Ontario over Sunday Observance. The
Jews and Seventh Day Adventists asked for recognition of the fact that
they worshipped on Saturday instead of Sunday. This was denied on the
grounds that "one day of rest in seven" was being granted on "secular"
grounds. (The new priests--the psychologists, psychiatrists and effi-
ciency experts--had declared that it was a good thing!) I asked one
Protestant member of the committee, which had worked out the grand consensus among representatives from government, supermarkets, labour
unions, churches, etc., what the Jews and Seventh Day Adventists
thought of this consensus. He replied that they were still hung up on
the idea that it was a religious holiday. I suggested that his church
would find renewed interest in the "religious" aspects if this legis-.
lation and in the rights of Christians as a group if the "secular" consensus decreed that the "one day of rest" should fall on Wednesday.

It is a sociological truism to say that as long as there is continuity between our identities and changes in society we remain un-
threatened and unconcerned about the impact of secular changes on our
religious practices. But the reverse is also true. Threats to our
identities bring into view our assumptions about how our religion should
function in relation to those identities. As a student of religion I
find my antennae twitching when I see evidence of threatened identities.
This is happening to some extent in relation to the multiculturalism
debate, but, as I have already said, this debate seems to be taking
place well within the reigning Canadian consensus. It is the persons
who are resisting that policy, and the perpetrators of racist attacks,
rather than the politicians, journalists, academics and church persons
who are promoting it and attacking racism, who fall outside of that
consensus. Where I do find identities being threatened is in relation
to questions of northern development, Native rights, nuclear energy policies, investments in South Africa and Chile, and Canada's relations
with the Third World. The common thread running through all of these

issues is the tension between supporters and critics of our industrial-
technological way of life. The Anglo-Saxon Protestant churches find
this debate raging within their communities.

A full account of the church activities which are now generating
such an impassioned response from the business community, as well as
from the clergy and others who share the businessmen's basic standpoint,
is beyond the scope of this paper.[19] Let me simply remind you that the
smoldering controversy between church leaders and businessmen was fanned
into an open flame when the churches appeared before the Berger Inquiry
and the National Energy Board in support of the Natives' demand for a
moratorium on the Northern pipeline. This brought the churches' cri-
tique of capitalism closer to home and made it more obviously political
than had the churches' other activities on behalf of a new international
economic order. I might suggest in passing that if the debate between
church leaders and businessmen is well under way in Toronto, the ancient
seat of capitalist power, it must be raging in Calgary, the new Jerusalem for the entrepreneurial spirit.)

This controversy between church leaders and Christian businessmen
reflects both the ambiguity of the religious practice of the Protestant
churches in modern Canada, and the recurrent nature of social activism
within the churches. As Richard Allen points out in his excellent history of the social gospel movement in Canada, the Protestant churches
were polarized during the 1920s as well into factions supporting and
attacking the industrial system.[20] The 1930s were also characterized by
debates between Christian socialists and defenders of the capitalist
economic and social order.[21] Once again active minorities within the
churches are on the side of the dissenters in relation to the reigning
consensus. That is, they are in solidarity with the critics of the
acquisitiveness and the unrestrained exploitation of non-renewable
natural resources which characterize industrial society. They are calling for a new social order based on cooperation and harmony with nature.
Just as in the 1930s when the radical wing of the churches joined the
effort to build a "cooperative commonwealth", the social activists of
the 1970s are aligned with the forces promoting a new international economic order and a "conserver" or "sustainable" society. For insiders
participating in this activity this is what appears to be consistent
with Christian teachings. For outsiders and critics of these actions,
the churches appear to be allowing themselves to be used by political
groups. Defenders and critics alike acknowledge that identification
with the causes of natives, socialists and conservationists, involves

the typically Protestant danger of sectarianism. That is, it courts the
risk of allowing sectarian alienation from the established order to become the stance that replaces the earlier church-type accommodation to
the dominant interests. These "sectarian" and "church-like" groups have
different perceptions of the chief danger confronting the churches. The
activists fear accommodation to the *status quo*, and thus risk being sectarian in their support of the causes of disadvantaged minorities.
Their critics are most worried about these sectarian tendencies, and
thus risk continued conformity to existing structures of power and privilege in their attempt to remain respectable and realistic.

In order to move below the abstract level of these mutual accusa-
tions of alienation and accommodation it is necessary to develop more
precise ways of identifying the means by which existing identities are
sacralized and proposals for change are legitimated. Since challenges
to an existing consensus must be explicitly defended, it is easier to
see which causes the church activists are legitimating than it is to
see how the dominant identity is being sacralized. For critics of the
industrial system, however, the use of phrases such as "the free enterprise system", "the profit motive", "economic growth", "the inevitable
expansion of technologically advanced societies", etc., provides evidence of a sacralized identity. Similarly, criticisms of Justice
Berger's method of inquiry and his recommendations provide intimations
of the way the dominant industrial identity is grounded in deeply rooted
convictions about the nature of man and society, and about what we
should trust in order to "solve" our "problems".

A great deal more work needs to be done in this area to render
these comments about the sacralization of identities, etc. intelligible
to persons who remain convinced that their positions are based simply on
"the facts", common sense, and a concern for the "public interest". This
clarification will, I expect, become even more important during the next
few years. It is going to become increasingly clear that what is at
stake is not merely the presence or absence of adequate information, but
fundamental judgments about the kind of society Canadians think is both
possible and consistent with our highest values. This is the confronta-
tion I now see taking place at the level of our symbol system. It is
still an open question, however, how the Protestant churches will appear
in retrospect to have functioned during this transitional period in our
history.

There are different possibilities regarding the role of the Protestant churches. On the one hand, the current controversy could prompt

the church leaders to pull back from their present practice of taking
sides in political disputes over issues such as the northern pipeline.
The Protestant churches could retreat to a cult-like preoccupation with
individual salvation or peace of mind. It is hard to see how they
could do this, however, without betraying their traditions of social
responsibility. On the other hand, they could discover renewed vigour
in the old role of sanctifying the identities of those who define Canada
as an industrial society made great by the profit motive and the free
enterprise system. This return to a "national church" mentally would,
in my view, involve sacralizing an identity increasingly in conflict
with the conviction that mutuality is the law of life for persons and
nations, and with the economic and social realities of the 1970s.

In the struggle to avoid sectarian alienation from or church-like
accommodation to the existing social order, the churches are experimenting with new ways of exerting a transforming impact upon industrial
society. It is perhaps not mere speculation and wishful thinking on my
part to suggest that in recent years the mainline Protestant churches
have re-emphasized their social responsibility without returning to a
"national church" self-image. There seems to be a new convergence of
religious groups with church-type and sectarian backgrounds. This time,
however, it seems to me that the churches are becoming more self-consciously "denominations." They are cooperating as equals with one
another, and with smaller groups, in a post-Christendom society, and
abandoning the "national church" mentality which characterized the
period of "voluntary Christendom."[22]

I do not mean to imply, however, that the Canadian churches are becoming denominations in the American sense as equal participants in the
task of balancing interests within the liberal consensus. The Canadian
denominations retain the conviction rooted in their church-type and sectarian origins that they have a divinely-ordained commission to witness
to a truth which is public and not merely private or therapeutic. They
differ from the earlier church-type natural law tradition, however, in
their assumptions about how this truth is known and the basis upon which
it should be enforced by civil authorities.[23]

Whether the Canadian Protestant churches return to their church-
type defence of an Anglo-Protestant Canada, become more self-consciously
pluralistic in relation to other interests being balanced within the
liberal consensus, or align themselves with other minorities in the
struggle for a new social order, will depend upon the relative success
of the factions they now embrace. My own hope is that they follow the

third path, and there are signs that this is happening. There is a new
coming together of large and small groups, just as when the Church of
England and the Methodists modified their church-type and sectarian
origins after the 1850s to promote the emerging liberal Protestant consensus. In the 1970s, the "big five", that is, the United, Anglican,
Presbyterian, Lutheran and Roman Catholic denominations, now cooperate
as equals with smaller groups such as the Mennonites and Quakers in
the Church Council on Justice and Corrections, and the Committee on
Justice and Liberty in Project North. Once again the church-type and
sectarian backgrounds of the different groups will provide a complementary mix. By learning from one another's histories of accommodation
and dissent they might find the proper balance in concrete situations
between sacralizing existing identities and legitimating criticisms of
identities which justify and render acceptable unjust and destructive
institutions and practices.

In conclusion, let us recall W. B. Creighton's remark about the
importance of groups which strive to articulate the relationship between
their actions and their religious convictions. In relation to assimilating non-Anglo-Saxons in the 1920s he pointed out that: "Neither the
schools nor the workshop, nor the mart, go down to the deepest springs
of life. Our religious feelings and interests reach down to what is
deepest in our common manhood, and it is on this sacred ground that we
are drawn most closely and sympathetically together."

To understand the role of religion and ethnicity in relation to
public issues such as multiculturalism and northern development in the
1970s, it is necessary to reverse Creighton's claim. Not only do our
religious feelings and interests reach down to what is deepest in our
common humanity. Our deepest feelings and interests about humanity reveal what is sacred for us, and thus points toward what our religion
really is. This empirical question of what we take for granted to be
unquestionably true, is the starting point for inter-faith dialogue with
those who do not share our denominational label, but who share important
aspects of our religion. It is also a good starting point for conversations with those who share our denominational label, but who are living
out a fundamentally different religion.

In response to the businessmen's demand that church activists get
their facts straight, the latter are inviting the former to reflect upon
their deepest feelings about the nature and purpose of human existence.
Together they can then ask how the feelings of both sides relate to the
aspects of their identities which they accept as unquestionably valid.

Perhaps on that sacred ground they will, as Creighton suggests, be
"drawn most closely and sympathetically together."

FOOTNOTES

1   Howard Palmer, ed., *Immigration and the Rise of Multiculturalism* (Toronto: Copp Clark Publishing, 1975), p. 112.

2   Cited in William Ormsby, "Lord Durham and the Assimilation of French Canada", in Norman Penlington, ed., *On Canada: Essays in Honour of Frank H. Underhill* (Toronto: University of Toronto Press, 1971), p. 39.

3   *Identity and the Sacred: A Sketch for a new social-scientific theory of religion* (Agincourt, Canada: The Book Society of Canada Limited, 1976), pp. 1, 5 and 6.

4   *Journal of the Canadian Church Historical Society*, Vol. XI, No. 3 (September, 1969), p. 60.

5   Robert Handy, *A History of the Churches in the United States and Canada* (Oxford University Press, 1977). See also John Webster Grant's article, "At least you knew where you stood with them: reflections on religion and pluralism in Canada and the United States", *Studies in Religion*, Vol. II, No. 4 (Spring, 1973), pp. 340-351.

6   "His Dominion: A Vision in Crisis", *Studies in Religion*, Vol. II, No. 4 (Spring, 1973), p. 315.

7   Cited in Clifford, p. 320.

8   Clifford, p. 320.

9   See Allan Smith, "Metaphor and Nationality", *Canadian Historical Review*, Vol. LI, No. 3 (September, 1970), pp. 247-275; and the article by John Webster Grant referred to above in note 5.

10 For a more extended discussion of the tendency of social scientists to stress the separation of religion from public policy in modern society see my paper, "Religion, Law and Morality in Modern Society." This paper was written for the Church Council on Justice and Corrections and will be published in Peter Slater's forthcoming collection of essays, *Religion and Culture in Canada/Religion et Culture au Canada* (Waterloo: Wilfred Laurier University Press, [1977]).

11 *Group Settlement: Ethnic Communities in Western Canada* (Toronto: Macmillan, 1936), pp. 293-294.

12 Dawson, p. 380.

13 Dawson, p. xvii.

14 Representative works of these scholars are, respectively: *The Scientific Study of Religion* (New York: Macmillan, 1970); *The Invisible Religion: The Problem of Religion in Modern Society* (New York: Macmillan, 1967);

The Denominational Society: A Sociological Approach to Religion in American Society (Glenview, Illinois: Scotte-Foresmand and Company, 1972);
Identity and the Sacred; Religion and Alienation: A Theological Reading of Sociology (New York and Toronto: Paulist Press, 1975).

15 "Mainline Protestantism in Canada and the United States: An Overview", (Unpublished Paper Presented at a Conference on Comparative Religious Organization: The United States and Canada, University of Waterloo, Waterloo, Ontario, May 1, 1977), pp. 24-25.

16 Palmer, p. 112.

17 Cited in Palmer, p. 133.

18 Cited in Palmer, pp. 136-137.

19 I am referring primarily to the activities of inter-church projects such as ICPOP (the Inter-Church Project on Population), the Task Force on the Churches and Corporate Responsibility, Project North (the Inter-Church Project on Northern Development), and GATT-fly.

20 *The Social Passion: Religion and Social Reform in Canada, 1914-1928* (Toronto: University of Toronto Press, 1972).

21 See my article, "The Canadian Social Gospel in the Context of Christian Social Ethics", in Richard Allen, ed., *The Social Gospel in Canada* (Ottawa: National Museum of Man Mercury Series, History Division, Paper No. 9, 1975), pp. 286-316.

22 In addition to Grant's article referred to above, see Tom Sinclair-Faulkner, "'For Christian Civilization': The Churches and Canada's War Effort, 1939-1942", (Ph.D. Thesis, The Divinity School, The University of Chicago, 1975).

23 For a fuller discussion of this point see my paper, "Religion Morality and Law in Modern Society", referred to above in note 10.

RELIGION AND WELSH NATIONALITY

The past conditions the present, not least in the development of
national consciousness and without memory nationality would wither.
Some would welcome such a prospect. Others, who value diversity, would
be appalled at the thought of a world unity reduced to a dull uniformity. Those who wish to retain a diversity of entities within the basic
unity of mankind see the fostering of nationality and the spirit of
internationalism not as contradictory endeavours in conflict but as
complementary activities. But what is nationality? It is hard to
agree on any single objective criterion. Race, language, a common territorial area, each has been advanced as the tap-root of national consciousness. But race and tribe have been mixed in the making of nations; different nations may share a language or an individual nation
may be bilingual, or even multilingual as in the case of Switzerland,
while the Jews retained their identity when they had no territorial
area. National consciousness can exist where there is an admixture of
different ingredients varying in permutation from instance to instance.
In case "A" it might be a common economic administration plus a territorial area; in "B" it might be a territorial area plus a common language while in "C" it might simply be the will and aspiration of the
people conjoined with a memory of past history.

A common heritage can bind a group together, or, to be more precise, an awareness of a common heritage can. Nationality has both an
inward and an outward reference, namely an awareness of a legacy which
spans the generations. To be pronounced this must be shared by a good
proportion of the populace. This awareness is unconsciously nurtured
when a people are constantly exposed to symbols of national identity,
such as images on the coins they handle, the stamps they use, the national anthem on their radio, etc.[1] On the other hand groups denied a
similar exposure, especially those overwhelmed by a powerful neighbour,
may discover that their awareness of identity diminishes and may dis-
appear unless they promote their own symbols. Wales in fact has developed its own cultural symbols such as the National Eisteddfod (A
Cultural Festival), the Welsh League of Youth, etc. The Welsh language
too has provided a continuum from Ancient Britain to the present with
a legacy of written literature from the eighth century. Yet in modern
Wales there is a deprived majority of Welsh people who have no knowledge

of the ancient tongue and no access to the treasury of literature.
Language is more than a means of communication--in this case it is a
thread which binds nearly two millenia of history. It is a nation's
memory. When this is endangered and threatened with extinction, the
other symbols of nationhood in due course will also be in jeopardy and
a people's distinctiveness will be lost. Those who resent this decline
may come to the view that the only way it can be halted is through se-
curing the right to handle their own affairs, that is by setting up
structures in education and in the arts, and strengthening rural communities, etc. This trend can be discerned in Wales in this century.
An increased awareness of national identity led to a renewed emphasis
upon cultural nationalism, but since the Second World War there is an
increase in the numbers of those who maintain that cultural nationalism
is a non-starter without the political structure to sustain it. As an
eminent Welsh historian once said, "nationalism is more than an awareness of nationality...it is a deliberate assertion thereof, and a conscious direction of effort towards some external manifestation which is
conceived, rightly, or wrongly, to be essential to the well being of
the nation."[2] Nationalism is growing in Wales particularly since
Plaid Cymru (Welsh Nationalist Party) gained its first parliamentary
seat in a by-election in 1966. The term nationalism, unfortunately,
has acquired a pejorative connotation since the days of the tyrranical
dictatorial nationalisms of the first half of this century. It did not
have such an obnoxious flavour, say, in the time of Gladstone or at the
time of Liberal radicalism. No nation has the right to oppress another,
or to misuse another; where that happens nationalism has become expan-
sionist and imperialist. Welsh nationalism has had no such aspirations
and its leaders have been dedicated to pacifist principles. It would
seem that the appeal of cultural survival is still much stronger within
it than political survival, although as stated a growing number can see
these as twin pillars upholding a nation's identity.

Since awareness of the legacy of the past seems to be an important
ingredient in nationality, the nation's history, myths, legends, epics
will acquire almost the status of a *heilsgeschichte*. Strangely enough
there has been comparatively little historical reference in the literary
tradition of Wales.[3] The emergence of national consciousness came from
a new interest in tradition, history, music and literature in the
eighteenth century; in the following century it was expressed in terms
of non-conformist radicalism, and in the present century largely in
cultural institutions. The modern era has produced its hero figures,

and also its poets with a fervent appeal to patriotism. One of the
most radical, Gwenallt, has emphasized the responsibility that goes
hand in hand with privilege, and his poetry has exercised considerable
influence.

To understand the contemporary scene it is necessary, however
briefly, to recall some events of significance in the nation's journey.

Who are the Welsh?

The Welsh are descendants of an Indo-European group designated the
Celtae by classical authors. By the Christian era one branch of the
Celts called the Brythoniaid (Britons) had settled in different parts of
the British Isles including Wales. Towards the end of the Roman occupation, at the time of the early Anglo-Saxon settlement, one form of the
British language became recognisable as Welsh.[4] It was spoken in parts
of Scotland, in parts of England as well as in Wales itself. By the
eighth century, it was a written language and in basics not very different from modern Welsh. Not without justification then has it been called by Professor Tolkien the Senior language of British civilization.[5]

The term "Welsh" is an Anglo-Saxon word derived from Wealh meaning
a foreigner in general. It survives in the word "walnut", which meant
literally a "foreign nut".[6] The term *wealh* was applied by the Anglo-
Saxon newcomers to the native population, whereas the descendants of
the Ancient Brythoniaid (Britons) referred to themselves in their own
language as Cymry, which means "brothers" or "fellow-countrymen", con-
veying the sense of a warm relationship. The same element, derived from
Cumbroges, occurs in the word Cumberland. Welsh may be the oldest living language of British civilization, but it struggles these days to
keep its foothold even in Wales, while outside Wales, elsewhere in Britain, no provision is made for offering the language as an option in
school curricula. Most people would be appalled at the temerity of anyone who might suggest the inclusion of this most truly British element
in an English syllabus!

Looking Backwards

The strong individualism of the Welsh character has been much in
evidence from early times. The partisanship of tribalism militated
against a sense of unity of solidarity. Once or twice some measure of
consolidation was achieved as under Llywelyn Fawr (1173-1240) and even
more so under Owain Glyndŵr (1402) who had aspirations for a national
parliament. The notions of "nation" and "nationality" were never as
strong as the sense of locality in medieval times, with some exceptions

such as among the clerics of the monasteries. Yet in spite of this the
Welshness of Wales was retained. It survived the triumph of Edward I
and the Norman Conquest but all but succumbed to the policies of that
enigmatic Welshman Henry Tudor and his successors on the English throne.
Henry Tudor fought under the banner of the Red Dragon at Bosworth and
whipped up the patriotism of the Welsh. Yet through his victory Wales
was reduced to a principality and the Act of Union of 1536 led to absorption. Most Welsh writers of today see the Act of Union as the betrayal of a nation. True, the Welsh were given some representation in
the English parliament but English law and administration were imposed
on Wales and the Welsh language outlawed in official and legal business.[7] It was the avowed policy of the Tudors to remove all distinction
as between Wales and England, particularly the Welsh language, and thus
in their opinion remove a severe handicap under which the Welsh labour-
ed. Even the translation of the Bible into the Welsh language was
meant to facilitate the acquiring of the English tongue that "such as
do not understand the language may, by conferring both tongues together,
the sooner attain to the knowledge of the English tongue". The policy
aimed at annexation and uniformity and Henry VIII decreed that "no person or persons that use the Welsh speech or language shall have or enjoy any Manner of Office or Fees within this realm of England, Wales or
other of the King's Dominion, upon pain of forfeiting the same offices
or Fees, unless he or they use and exercise the English Speech of
Language".[8] The Welsh aristocracy were absorbed by the English ruling
circles and by the end of the Tudor period the assimilation of Wales
would have been complete but for the conservativism and tenacity of the
peasantry. As so often in the history of religions and nations the ordinary people retained and treasured what officialdom rejected. The
translation of the Bible had an unexpected result. It gave the Welsh a
sublime standard for its language. This had not been foreseen but it is
possible that Welsh would have disappeared but for the 1588 translation.

The language question has been a barometer of national consciousness ever since. Strong feelings were aroused by what is referred to as
the Betrayal of the Blue Books. Here was another attempt to eliminate
the Welsh language, or at least to restrict its use most severely. The
Blue Books comprise the report of the Royal Commission of Inquiry into
the State Education in Wales in 1847. Members of the Commission were
not even linguistically equipped to assess the educational scene and had
to rely upon second-hand accounts from prejudiced witnesses. Yet this
did not deter them from wholesale condemnations of the educational

system and from attempting to destroy the language, which was referred
to as "that disastrous barrier to all moral improvement and proper progress in Wales". The report was seen as an attack not only upon the
language but also as a defamatory racist document which only succeeded
in making the Welsh more conscious of their nationhood.[9] The report
called for English to be the sole medium of instruction in Wales and
brought about the infamous "Welsh Not". This was a wooden device sus-
pended by a string and put around a child's neck when he or she was
caught speaking the native tongue. (Bretons were subject to a similar
practice in France.) The report attacked not only the educational system and the language but also the Non-Conformist religion to which it
attributed most of the ills of the day. Unfortunately the very person
whom the report attacked adopted the policy and recommendation of the
report and the result was the complete anglicisation of the educational
system from primary to higher education.[10]

It would be quite erroneous, however, to give the impression that
religion in general and non-conformity in particular had a stultifying
effect upon the growth of national consciousness. The opposite is the
case as I shall endeavour to show. In fact the Welsh identity has always been at its strongest when the "Welsh" Christian Faith has been at
its deepest.[11]

If Welsh consciousness had been largely dissipated by the seven-
teenth century, the next century brough reinvigouration when religious
and educational movements had a concerted impact upon it. The Methodist Religious Revival of the eighteenth century stimulated the Welsh
consciousness and formed the refreshing stream which flowed into the
older river of dissent.[12] On the educational side the circulating
schools of Gruffydd Jones whose primary aim had been religious, enabled
thousands to cross the frontier of literacy. It is estimated that before he died in 1761 over 158,000 had been taught in his schools. It
had been his view that the destruction of the Welsh language would be
tantamount to defying the disposition of divine Providence.[13] The
Methodist Revival led to cultural benefits and language stimulation
also, it occasioned a prolific literary output and produced some of the
best known of hymns. Its language was entirely Welsh and its leaders'
names are still revered in homes where religion still means something.
One of its most eminent personalities was William Williams of Pantycelyn
"a master in the realm of Christian praise" but no mean scholar either.[14] The Methodist Revival made a mute nation articulate, according
to R. T. Jenkins,[15] while the Welsh novelist Emyr Humphreys says that in

the adult schools of the Methodist eighteenth century the Welsh became
one of the first literate peasantries in Europe. Of the chapels, he
said, "They were part of a network of little democracies where the ancient language found a new outlet of expression and a new strength".[16]
By way of contrast the Anglican Church in Wales was hostile to the new
religious enthusiasm and indifferent to the language. In fact from
1715 to 1870 not a single Bishop in Wales could speak the language.
Even as late as 1886 a Bishop of St. David's could dismiss Wales as
merely a "geographical expression". Matthew Arnold had already called
for one homogeneous English speaking whole in Britain, regarding the
Welsh language as a nuisance. He was by no means alone.[17]

The Methodist Revival turned Wales into a vigorous non-conformity
by the beginning of the nineteenth century. That century was the gold-
en era of non-conformity, so much so that Gladstone could remark in
1891 "the non-conformists of Wales are the people of Wales".[18] It was
also the century which saw the rise of Welsh self-consciousness and
this is reflected in Welsh-language denominational literature and in
poetry. The century produced non-conformist leaders of calibre like
Emrys ap Iwan, Thomas Gee, and Michael D. Jones now regarded as Fathers
of Nationalism. Even that enigmatic spell-binder David Lloyd George
was attracted by the Home-rule movement of 1886-1895, only to oppose the
Home-rule bill in 1921. In the early years of this century interest
in Home-rule declined, and it was all but forgotten during the First
World War. It was raised in Parliament again in 1943, during the Second
World War, and the first "Welsh Day" for debate was introduced a year
later.

The Contemporary Scene

Up until the sixties, agitation for a Welsh Parliament had been in
fairly low key and primarily motivated by a desire to halt further cultural erosion. Since then, there is an increasing disinclination to
separate the issues of cultural and political identity, particularly
among the younger generation. Some feel that the older members of Plaid
Cymru, the Nationalist Party, have been too culture conscious and too
little aware of economic, industrial and political issues. The Nationalist cause has strong support in non-conformist circles. Plaid Cymru's
declared aim is freedom rather than separation. Its basic tenet is that
Wales is a nation and has the right and need to rule its own house, to
have adequate representation in the European Parliament and its own
voice in the international sphere, that is, in the United Nations. In

fact during the sixties the annual assemblies of the Congregationalists, the Baptists, and the North Wales Presbyterians all passed resolutions supporting Home-rule. The religious factor may not be as pronounced as in the last century but it is by no means insignificant. The former President of Plaid Cymru has been Chairman of the Union of Welsh Independents; three Principals of three theological colleges have been parliamentary candidates for Plaid Cymru. Leading ministers who are not politically involved have declared support for the concept of national identity. For instance Dr. Martyn Lloyd Jones of Westminster Chapel, London, said in an interview: "Every nation is given the opportunity to manifest particularly God's glory in a manner which no other nation can; our obvious duty then is to preserve our national distinction."[19] The non-conformists, however, are by no means the only religious groups in sympathy with nationalistic aspirations. Two Bishops have declared support for Home-rule and Archbishops have made interventions in the political debate. Mr. Saunders Lewis one of the founders of Plaid Cymru and the most-listened-to elder on the Welsh scene is a Catholic. Behind his policies lies a Christian view of society.[20] For him, the nation, like a person, has a duty derived directly from the divine imperative. Others have vehemently attacked this foundation for nationality. Dr. Iorwerth Peate, who has done so much for the preservation of folk culture in Wales, sees great dangers in the notion of the sanctity of a nation. In his view God has not ordained nor consecrated any nation. A nation, he argues, does not possess a soul nor a conscience nor a moral personality. It has never been an essential part of Christianity.[21] Peate supports national identity on other grounds and favours this definition of nationality: "a form of corporate consciousness of peculiar intensity, intimacy and dignity, related to a definite home country".[22] In fact practically every shade of theological opinion can be found in Wales in the Post-War era but the assertion of nationality cuts across theological and denominational divisions.

If church attendance is any criterion of power, the power of non-conformity has certainly dwindled in the Post-War era. In the same period nationalism has grown in appeal. This has produced an interesting situation in which older leaders steeped in religious traditions are found working for the same political goals as an apparently religion-less generation. Whereas the former were prevented from anything approaching violent action by pacifist principles, the young may not be as inhibited, although so far they too have chosen to avoid conflict and have concentrated upon civil disobedience. This has been true also of the Language Society which is the most active on the Welsh scene. This was founded in 1962 as the result of a broadcast by the veteran Saunders Lewis on the need to save the language and to use it in official and administrative capacities. Nuisance damage has been done to selected government targets but the perpetrators almost in each case give themselves up voluntarily after making their protest. The attitude of the religious leaders to this group and its activities is illustrated in a study by P. J. Madgwick in Cardiganshire, a predominantly Welsh-speaking area. Thirty-seven ministers were interviewed. Three out of four of them had Welsh as their first language, and twenty-nine expressed concern for the language. One in four showed virtually unqualified sympathy for the Welsh Language Society; two in four sympathized with the aims but not the methods of the Society, and one in four or less were unsympathetic or critical.[23] It cannot be overlooked that the roots of this generation of language defenders are also deep in the religious traditions which inspired radical liberalism in the last century, Labour in this, and now Nationalism. Most of the Language Society members have been brought up in religious circles. Religion is also a foundational principle of the Non-political Welsh Youth Organization (YR Urdd) with its threefold loyalites: "To Wales, to Fellow-Man, to Christ". This movement has done tremendous good work for the cultural benefit of several generations of young people since its inception fifty years ago.

Religion has been a formative influence in most Welshmens' lives in the past determining attitudes, inspiring literature and leading to social action.[24] The power-house of dissent has generated a tremendous moral force, but that power is sadly on the wane. The religious communities, particularly the chapels, have preserved the language and this is now the centre of controversy, the focal point of action and the fermenting agent of national consciousness and conscience. I cannot share the view that dissatisfaction with the economic position of Wales vis-à-vis the United Kingdom has ousted the quest for cultural survival from its position of priority.[25] For most, especially the young, the language is more important than the price of beef.

The Language

The language question is the rallying point for defenders of national identity and the central political issue of this decade. In the past religion has come to its rescue when government and administration rejected it. The Protestant reformers "succeeded in wedding a devotion

to the Scriptures with the emotive and patriotic inheritance of language".[26] Later that unique institution, The Adult Sunday School in
Wales preserved the language and promoted faith and education at the
same time, ever since the Methodist Revival. It was only in the domain
of religion the participants were free to use their own language "without having to fight battles with an intransigent bureaucracy".[27]

     Today the religious connection is weak and the question of the sur-
vival of the language is more acute than ever and the situation more
precarious. There are many who feel that national identity will disap-
pear with the disappearance of the language, for Wales has no other institution such as a special faith, or law, which could save it from total assimilation. An encouraging feature is a strong identity-wish a-
mong a good number of the non-Welsh-speaking. One of the major tasks
ahead is to promote harmony and deepen the relationship between this
majority and the Welsh-speaking minority. The number of Welsh-speakers
has declined drastically in this century and most steeply of all in the
Post-War era. Educational policies, migrations, industralisation, mobility and not least the media--all these are contributory factors. In
1891, 54.4% of the population were Welsh-speakers. By now the Welsh
speakers count for a little over 20% of the population. In a predominantly Welsh-speaking county like Carmarthenshire, 86% of the children
spoke Welsh, now it is about 36%. Yet there continue to be some areas
where the number is as high as 75% e.g. in parts of Cardiganshire, where
half the population is also non-conformist.[28]

     The language struggle has shown that many of the young are prepared
to sacrifice property, time and career until Welsh is given official
status in law, education and administration and that without hindrance,
that is, *de facto* as well as *de jure*. Emyr Humphreys finds that the
language issue, "means, among many other things, that the persistent
altruistic strain in the Welsh tradition which created Welsh non-conformity and indeed Welsh Socialism has found a new outlet".[29]

An Attempt At Culture Transplant: A venture linking Wales, Patagonia
and Saskatchewan.

     Outside his own country the Welshman has integrated successfully
in his adopted society. One of the reasons is that he has not emigrated
in groups sufficiently strong in numbers to sustain his identity, and he
has been easily absorbed. This does not mean that there have been no
attempts at all to set up Welsh ethnic groups. In the Western Hemi-
sphere--Newfoundland, Brazil, Pennsylvania, Philadelphia, Tennesee,

Virginia--each of these has attracted Welsh immigrants who had hopes of
forming a small Welsh community. The story of the emigration of Welsh
Quakerism to Pennsylvania has been the theme of a couple of successful
Welsh historical novels in recent years and Dr. Pennar Davies describes
that emigration as "one of the most promising products of Puritan ex-
uberance" and a loss to Wales.[30] The story of the Welsh in the United
States has not gone unnoticed and attention has been called to the vigour of their churches in many of which Welsh was the medium of worship
well into this century, and also to the output of Welsh books and literature from American publishers which was quite impressive considering
the limited readership. At one time in Ohio alone there were scores of
Welsh churches, and I was privileged to officiate six years ago in the
100th anniversary of the formation of the association of one such group
in Gallia County. None of these churches is now Welsh-speaking, and
the last of the Welsh churches in the United States where Welsh services
were held regularly was the one in New York, and that closed its doors
a few years ago. As far as I know occasional Welsh language services
are now held only in Chicago, Los Angeles and Beavers' Creek in the
United States, while in Canada the only church where Welsh language services can be heard regularly, (twice a month, in fact) is the Dewi Sant
Church in Toronto; I shall have more to say about this church presently.

    The emigration which has captured the imagination of the Welsh more
than any other was not to North America but to Patagonia in South America, which turned out to have links with Canada as well. The original
intention was to found a new independent Welsh national state, but this
ambition was never realized. Principal Michael D. Jones of the Bala
Theological College, already referred to as one of the Fathers of Welsh
Nationalism, had been as a young man, for three years or so, a minister
of the Welsh Church in Cincinatti, Ohio. He had been distressed to find
that so few links existed between the widely separated Welsh groups in
North America, with the consequent weakening of the hold which national
identity exercised upon the scattered groups. He was even more distressed at the erosion of Welsh culture at home, the increase in Anglicisation, and the oppressiveness of landlords. He had a vision of a
Welsh colony in a new land, far from landlord domination and the pressure of established religion. In fact the Welsh Society in California
had mooted the idea of a Welsh Colony in 1858 and invited him over, but
the Civil War intervened. A decade earlier a hundred Welshman had emigrated with a group of merchants to Brazil, but the whole venture had
proved to be a dismal failure, and this memory was no help to the new

enterprise. However, in 1861 a Welsh colonization society was set up in
Liverpool. Various possible locations were discussed but the choice
fell upon Patagonia. Here Michael D. Jones hoped the new Wales would
flourish and that the language of chapel, school and parliament would
be Welsh, while at the same time the community would endeavour to be a
blessing to the whole of the Argentine. Argentina in fact had been
calling for settlers[31] but the problem was that both Chile and Argentine
claimed jurisdiction over the area selected and this led to many com-
plications subsequently. Patagonia was described by the secretary of
the Colonization Society in Liverpool as "a fertile land whose topo-
graphy was not dissimilar to that of Wales".[32] The enthusiasm was genuine and Michael D. Jones's sincerity beyond questions for his wife's
money financed the Colonization society.[33]

The first group of 150, consisting primarily of quarrymen and min-
ers, left Wales for the Chubut River area in 1864 and the story of their
heroic struggles, in what turned out to be a no-man's land, rivals that
of most early settlers. More emigrants followed, but by the late 1880s
the flow had practically ceased. The story that follows is one of tension and struggle as the Argentinians urged assimilation, with Spanish
as the official language, and the Welsh tried very hard to withstand it.
In fact they found themselves once again a minority engaged in struggles which were all too familiar. In the 1890s there were many disputes
over land titles, education, and over army service. Most of the Welsh
were non-conformists with strict sabbatarian views. They objected to
military training on the day set aside for worship and what was for them
the means of community renewal. Their objection was not entirely in
vain but even so the force of erosion grew stronger and one Governor
openly advocated one religion and one language for the whole country.
It is remarkable, to say the least, that while the idea of a Welsh colony was doomed to failure from the start, so much was achieved by so few.
They *did* set up their chapels, and schools; they transplanted the Eisteddfod and even in adversity managed to publish their own monthly paper,
and above all they kept the language alive even to this day, if only
just.

A census in 1896 showed that there were twenty-five hundred people
in the Chubut Valley and a further two hundred in the Andean Piedmont.
A serious flood in 1899 devastated most of what had been built up over
the preceding years. Two years later another disastrous flood occurred.
The Canadian immigration agent had already been in contact with the
Pantagonian Welsh since 1892 and arrangements had been made for some to

migrate to the vicinity of Winnipeg. These came nearer implementation
after a visit to Western Canada by Mr. David Lloyd George. He encouraged the Welsh Patagonians to migrate to Canada and in February, 1902,
some thirty came and settled southwest of Saltcoats. Then on May 15,
of the same year, some two hundred and thirty left from Port Madryn on
the steamship Orissa for Liverpool, of whom nearly half were in their
twenties. Two hundred and eight continued the journey from Liverpool
to Canada on the steamship Numidian.

     The children of these immigrants were bilingual, that is, they
spoke Welsh and Spanish, but they had no English. What happened was
almost inevitable. These children soon became English-speaking, and
the following generation, "widely dispersed by a changing agricultural
economy", knew little if any Welsh.[34] The spiritual welfare of the new
community was ministered to by the Reverend David G. Davies, an Anglican, and the Reverend William T. Morris--a Congregationalist--both of
whom had been with the new-comers in Patagonia. Out of necessity, as
it were, there emerged a grass-roots ecumenism, for most of the immigrants were Calvinistic Methodists! The latter had no minister of their
own and they became affiliated later with the Welsh Presbyterian Church
of the United States which sent them a Welsh-speaking minister in 1912
and supported the Saskatchewan community as a mission field.[35] Bethel,
the Welsh Chapel in the Llewelyn district of the Saskatchewan Welsh Community had no Welsh services after 1936, except for the special anniversary service in 1952.

     While some of the early migrants still speak Welsh with remarkable
fluency and ease, and quote poetry liberally from memory,[36] in the case
of children this proficiency is sadly, but perhaps inevitably absent.
The same pattern of loss has been repeated recurrently in minority cultures. Even in the case of such strong Welsh communities outside Wales,
such as the London-Welsh community, it is the exception rather than the
rule for a person of the second generation within the community to be
Welsh-speaking,[37] and it is rare indeed for a member of the third generation to demonstrate knowledge of the language, although the establishing of the primary "Welsh medium schools" may change this situation
somewhat.

     After the Welsh-Patagonian migration in 1902 conditions seemed to
have improved in Wales itself, for the Commissioner for Canadian immigration complained in 1907 that the number of arrivals from Wales was
not anything like what was desired.[38] People continued to arrive in
Canada, however, particularly during the years of depression in the

twenties and thirties, but no rural communities have been established,
to the best of my knowledge, except for the one mentioned and another
in Ponoka, Alberta, which continues to draw people from Calgary and much
wider afield to its annual Gymanfa Ganu (Singing Festival) in August.[39]
Most emigrants from Wales over the years have found their way to the
cities, and in many of these centres there are Welsh Societies of varying degress of vitality. The only existing Welsh Church in the whole
of Canada, however, is the Dewi Sant Church in Toronto and it is to this
church I would like to turn my attention, now, at the end of this paper.

A Welsh Church In Canada

The Dewi Sant Church, Toronto, continues to provide Welsh-language
services twice a month in addition to the normal English-language service and the latter also will often include some Welsh hymns. It is
now within the United Church of Canada, but historically it is the child
of the Welsh revival of 1904-05 when immigrants brought the glow and
fervour of the revival with them to Toronto. A St. David's Society,
founded in 1906, already provided social contact and fellowship, but
"deep religious convictions - craved for expression in their mother
tongue".[40] The Church, named after the patron saint of Wales, "Dewi"
(David) was founded in 1909 as the Dewi Sant Welsh Presbyterian Church
in affiliation with the Welsh Presbyterian Church of the U.S.A. At that
time it would have been the focal point of a community which was largely
if not wholly Welsh-speaking, but by now "Dewi Sant" is described in an
official church pamphlet as "not predominantly Welsh in language but
Welsh in character". In fact even as early as 1918 it became necessary
to make some concession on the use of English in some of the services.
Today, the proportion attending the Welsh services is only one fourth of
the regular congregation attending the English medium services. The
intriguing question is why the non-Welsh speaking continue to travel,
many miles in most cases, to this city church, rather than one nearer
their homes.

In June of this year a questionnaire was distributed to some sixty
members.[41] Forty-seven questionnaires were returned, and replies indicated that thirty-seven respondents attend the Welsh church "regularly",
four "frequently" and the other six "sometimes". Twenty-one listed
Welsh as their first language. This was surprisingly high until one
looked at the age groups. Seventy-seven percent of those who gave their
ages were in the fifty-plus group and most of them had been in Canada
for over twenty years at least.

In response to the question: "Is your Welsh association important
to you?", Forty-three gave a firm affirmative and four replies "somewhat". Answers to questions on Ethnicity were distributed as follows:

	Yes	Somewhat	Not At All	No Answer
Do you think Ethnic identity important?	33	8	4	2

	Yes	No	Undecided	No Answer
Do you think Ethnic groups should be encouraged in Canada?	40	2	2	3
Do you think there is a place for Ethnic churches in Canada?	44	0	0	3
Do you think there is a place for a Welsh church in Canada?	44	1	0	2

All four who returned a definite "Not at all" to the first question:
"Do you think Ethnic identity important?", gave English as their first
language. Yet two had already affirmed the importance of their Welsh
association and the other two had indicated that it was "somewhat" important. One of these two gave very strong negative answers to all the
other "Ethnic" questions specified above and added the comment that
concern for Ethnic identity "contributes to racism; ghettos and unrest".
"Why live in the past? Why not build a better Canada with Canadians?"
The same respondent showed a wry sense of humour when he wrote in reply
to the question, "'What in your opinion constitutes a 'Welsh church?':"
--"A group of people who left Wales for a better life in Canada--and
spending most of their lives dreaming of Wales!". Unintentionally, perhaps, he shows how deep-seated the nostalgia of the Welsh is for the
land of their Fathers. The same question elicited a variety of interesting responses e.g.:--"A unique underlying Welsh spirit that permeates
relationships of even second and third generations," "promotion of culture", (says a non-Welsh speaker!); "atmosphere more than language"; "a
realistic recognition that it is part of the Canadian community but with
a distinctive language and culture"; "avoidance of nostalgia, and avoidance of 'power games'." A very high proportion stressed the importance
of good singing and relatively few the actual use of the Welsh language in the services.

This little exercise in relation to the Welsh church in Toronto was
not meant to be anything but a very cursory and preliminary investigation. It merits fuller examination as does the whole question of the
Welsh in Canada. A fuller treatment of the subject needs to correlate

the changing pattern of the religious life in Wales itself with the
changing behaviour of the immigrant. This is of course true of Welsh
churches and Welsh societies anywhere beyond Offa's Dyke. It is not
surprising that the new immigrants of today do not share the enthusiasm
of their older compatriots for the church when their link with religious institutions in an increasingly secularised Wales have been tenu-
ous in the homeland or even non-existent. The church or chapel is no
longer the focal centre for social fellowship and cultural pursuits as
in the past. The car, the box, and not least the practice of eating
out in pubs, has changed the social life of Wales. It is little wonder
that the immigrant in a new land does not anymore regard chapel attendance as a *sine qua non* of a full existence. Yet at the same time, as
in Wales itself, one detects a growing sense of ethnic identity and with
it a growing interest in the Welsh language. The present writer when
residing in Ottawa (1968-1973) conducted a Welsh class in his home.
This was attended by about ten people. Today, in the capital city, the
Welsh society runs three Welsh language classes for different compe-
tence - range groups. This growth of interest is not restricted to the
Ottawa area.

What the immigrant societies seem to lack is precisely what Michael
D. Jones complained about in the last century, namely adequate inter-
communication between widely separated groups, and even more so if ethnic identity is to be supported, closer contact with their cultural matrix, which the Welsh Patagonians have urged for over a century. This
is not to ignore the attempts that have been made through the link supplied by the bilingual publication for Welsh societies abroad *Yr Enfys*
(The Rainbow), the welcoming day at the Annual National Eisteddfod, and
recently the attempt to set up a Welsh youth link in North America.[42]

Can the immigrant live with his twin loyalties? My answer would
depend upon the strength of his roots in the first place. Where these
are strong both loyalties can be sustained even to the second generation but where the former commitment is weak, assimilation is naturally
swifter and more thorough. What does come through unmistakably in the
responses given by the Dewi Sant members is the recognition of the need
to integrate as fully as possible in the country where they now live,
irrespective of their former loyalty or their degree of attachment to
it. This is a worthy aspiration, be it for the immigrant in Wales, or
in Canada.

The paradoxical situation in Wales is that while the attraction of
religious institutions is in decline, awareness of nationality is

increasing especially among the young. In the past, as I have attempted to show, religion has nurtured national consciousness; now the latter seems to be on the road to secularization and makes its appeal increasingly independent of religious reference. This has been the way
of many religion-inspired social and political movements in the past.

FOOTNOTES

1 See J. R. Jones, "Y Syniad o Genedl" in *Efrydiau Athronyddol* XXIV (1961) 3-17 and *Cristnogaeth a Chenedlaetholdeb* (John Penry n.d.).

2 R. T. Jenkins, "The Development of Nationalism in Wales" in *The Sociological Review* XXVII (2) (April, 1935) pp. 163-182.

3 J. F. Rees, *The Problem of Wales and Other Essays* (University of Wales, 1963) p. 29.

4 Melville Richards, The Listener (Nov. 7, 1968).

5 See Emyr Humphreys, "The Welsh Condition" in *The Spectator* (March 28, 1970).

6 Melville Richards, *ibid.*

7 A. B. Philip, *The Welsh Question: Nationalism in Welsh Politics 1945-1970* (University of Wales Press, 1975).

8 See Wyn Griffith, *The Welsh* (1950).

9 R. Coupland, *Welsh and Scottish Nationalism: A Study* (London, 1954) p. 195.

10 Saunders Lewis, "The Fate of the Language" in A. R. Jones and G. Thomas, edits. *Presenting Saunders Lewis* (University of Wales, 1973).

11 Daniel Jenkins, *The British: Their Identity and Their Religion* (S.C.M., 1975) p. 53; R. Tudur Jones, *The Desire of Nations* (Christopher Davies, 1974).

12 Cf. Gwyn Williams in *Efrydiau Athronyddol* XXIV (1961) pp. 18-30.

13 See R. Tudur Jones, "The Welsh Language and Religion" in M. Stephens, edit., *The Welsh Language Today* (Gomer Press, 1973) p. 68.

14 See the writer's article, "The Unfeigned Faith and an Eighteenth Century Pantheologia" in *NUMEN* XV (3) (1968) pp. 208-217.

15 Quoted by W. Griffith, *op.cit.*

16 E. Humphreys, *ibid.*

17 Cf. the editorial in the *Times*, Sept. 8, 1866, quoted by H. Gruffudd, "Y Syniad o Genedl yn Uenyddiaeth Gymraeg yr Ugeinfed Ganrif", unpublished M.A. Thesis, University of Wales (1973).

18 Hansard, Feb. 20, 1891, p. 1265.

19 See also *Y Cylchgrawn Efengylaidd* VI (1965) pp. 108-109.

20   See D. M. Lloyd in W. Pennar Davies edit., *Saunders Lewis ei feddwl a'i waith* (Denbigh, 1950) p. 46.

21   *Ym Mhob Pen* (Aberystwyth, 1948) 30 cited by H. Gruffudd *op.cit.*

22   A. Zimmern, *Modern Political Doctrines* (Oxford, 1939).

23   P. J. Madgwick, et alia, *The Politics of Rural Wales* (London, 1973) 68 ff.

24   Cf. Coupland, *op.cit* p. 216.

25   For a contrary view see R. R. Corrado, "Nationalism and Communalism in Wales" in *Ethnicity* Vol. 2 (4) pp. 360-381.

26   R. Mathias, in M. Stephens edit., *The Welsh Language Today* pp. 42f.

27   R. Tudur Jones *ibid.*

28   Madgwick, *op.cit* p. 15.

29   Emyr Humphreys, *op.cit.*

30   W. T. Pennar Davies in R. Brinley Jones edit. *Anatomy of Wales* (1972) pp. 105-116.

31   *The Times* Sept. 8, 1856 p. 6, cited by Lewis H. Thomas, "From the Pampas to the Prairies: the Welsh Migration of 1902" in *Saskatchewan History* XXIV (No. 1) (Winter, 1971) p. 1.

32   See E. G. Bowen, "The Welsh Colony in Patagonia 1865-1885: A Study in Historical Geography" in *Geographical Journal* Vol. 132 (1966) pp. 16-31; Lewis H. Thomas, *op.cit* pp. 1-12.

33   Alun Davies, "Michael D. Jones a'r Wladfa" in *Trafodion Cymdeithas Anrhydeddus Y Cymrodorion 1966* i, pp. 73-87.

34   Lewis H. Thomas, *op.cit* p. 12.

35   Lewis H. Thomas, "Welsh Settlement in Saskatchewan, 1902-1904" in *The Western Historical Quarterly* IV(4) (Oct., 1973) p. 446.

36   See Gordon W. Maclennan, "A Contribution to the Ethno history of Saskatchewan's Patagonian Welsh Settlement" in *Canadian Ethnic Studies/Études ethniques du Canada* Vol. VIII 2 (1975) pp. 57-72, for translation and transcript of conversations between Mr. William Edward Jones and interviewer Mrs. Glenys James.

37   Fortunately there are good examples of those exceptions, and Mrs. James, mentioned in the previous note, is one, who although brought up in London, is immersed in Welsh culture and a fluent Welsh-speaker. She would be the first to recognize her debt in this respect to her Welsh church in London, frequent visits to Wales in her youth and participation in YR URDD (Welsh League of Youth). Today, a self-supporting bilingual school in London, and bilingual schools in the anglicized areas of Wales, afford further opportunity for nurturing cultural roots.

38   Lewis H. Thomas, *op.cit* p. 448.

39 *Ponoka*
    Welsh immigrants arrived in Ponoka at the turn of the century.
    Most of them came from the United States, from Minnesota, Wiscon-
    sin, and Nebraska, attracted by the opportunity to acquire home-
    steads in Alberta. Many had little or no previous knowledge of
    farms being artisans such as plasterers and bricklayers. Some did
    not remain.
    A Welsh Sunday School was formed in 1903 and two years later a
    church was formally established and was referred to as the Welsh
    Calvinistic Methodist Church of Magic. Perhaps I should add
    "Magic" was the name of the District. The Church was later affili-
    ated with the Welsh Presbyterian Church of the United States and
    remained so until 1939 when it merged with the United Church of
    Canada.
    In 1914 another church had been founded in Wood River and Welsh
    language services were held there until 1929. These services were
    ended because "Through the years many of the Welsh people passed
    away or moved to make their homes elsewhere, leaving very few to
    carry on the work, and making it unnecessary to continue in the
    Welsh language"...(*Mecca Glen Memories* (1968) Ponoka, Alta.,
    p. 194); see also W. Griff Jones, compiler, *Over the Years at Zion*
    (1974-1976) (Ponoka Herald.)
    On a recent visit to Ponoka I was informed that at one time there
    were some two hundred Welsh speaking persons in the settlement.
    Now it is a mere handful who can speak Welsh, but those who do,
    speak it well with the characteristic accents of the various places
    where their parents and grandparents had come from in North Wales.
    Inter-marriage with other ethnic groups and dispersion, these were
    given as reasons for the decline. What was surprising however was
    that some who continued to speak Welsh were second and even third-
    generation immigrants. They had kept the language alive by using
    it constantly at home. They confessed that most of them would find
    it difficult to follow a Welsh sermon and that most read no Welsh
    at all. While the first generation of settlers had read and writ-
    ten Welsh poetry, some with considerable skill, even intricate
    Welsh englynion, the remnant had lost such skills, but some had
    channelled a gift, no doubt inherited, into English verse. Here
    as elsewhere in North America, by this time, about the only Welsh
    institution left is the annual Gymanfa Ganu (Singing Festival).
    With the passing of the present generation, no more Welsh will be
    heard in Ponoka.

40 See J. Humphreys Jones, *A Short History of Dewi Sant Welsh United
    Church, Toronto, Canada* (1957) p. 6.

41 I am indebted to Miss Eluned M. Thomas (another "second- if not
    third-generation" product of the London-Welsh, community, now re-
    siding in Toronto) for her assistance in duplicating, distributing
    and collecting these questionnaires at very short notice.

42 W.A.Y. = Welsh Associated Youth of Canada and the United States.
    A good nucleus of the society, including the secretary Miss Myfanwy
    Davies, reside in Ottawa.

RELIGION AND ETHNICITY: AN OVERVIEW OF ISSUES RAISED

Although this is not the first conference on "Religion and Ethnicity" in Canada, it is unique in an important aspect. While there have
been many studies of the various aspects of "Christian Ethnicity" or at
most "Jewish and Christian Ethnicity", the uniqueness of this conference is found in its inclusiveness of some of the many religious ethnic
groups in Canada: Mennonite; Welsh; Roman Catholics of French, Ukrainian, Polish and Hungarian backgrounds; Japanese Pure Land Buddhism; and
Muslims of Lebanese, Palestinian, Arab, Egyptian, African, West Indian
and Indo-Pakistani extractions. In spite of this rich diversity, it
is evident that certain religious ethnic groups, e.g. the Canadian
Jews, were not featured in the discussion. Although a Jewish speaker
had been included in the planning of the conference, he found it necessary to withdraw at the last minute.

All participants at the conference agreed that the present period
is crucial in the life of this rich diversity of religious ethnic minorities existing in Canada today. The evidence presented indicates
that they are in danger of vanishing, of being either absorbed by the
dominant Anglo-Saxon culture or wiped out by the conformity induced by
the Twentieth Century technological society. It is without doubt a
time of testing for the religious ethnic minorities of Canada.

Although this conference is far from being the final word on the
problems of Canadian religious minority groups, it does present a useful beginning stage in the study of religion and ethnicity. From the
academic perspective a useful result of the conference was the emergence of points of common experience across the diversity of religious
ethnic groups studied. Of course there were some definite differences
as well, and these will be analyzed after the common experiences are
examined.

I. Points of Common Experience

1. The Search for Land and Wealth

In his paper introducing the Canadian scene at the turn of the century, David Goa pointed out that the first members of ethnic minorities
came to Canada in search of new land and the wealth it would bring.
This motivation for land and wealth was encouraged by the publications
originating in the office of the Minister of the Interior, the

Honourable Clifford Sifton. The cover of these publications was often adorned with a prairie goddess figure, with a few stems of well headed out wheat in her left hand and a horn of plenty in her right. She symbolizes the attraction that the promise of land and wealth exerted on the first wave of settlers. They came, in many cases, in search of land and wealth, and therefore were not always the most devout persons. Often their plan was to make a "bundle" as quickly as possible and then return home. It was the lure of riches which first drew to Canada Lebanese Muslims, Japanese Buddhists, Welsh Protestants and Polish Catholics. It is no surprise, therefore, that in these new ethnic communities, the religious developments were often slow in starting.

Although a few did manage to save a good sum of money and return home, the majority who came with that plan in mind never realized it. Many were unable to find high paying work and so found it impossible to realize their dream of returning home rich. And to return home poor meant a defeat and loss of face that few were willing to accept. So they stayed on and began to think of Canada in a more permanent fashion, transferring their hopes for financial success to the generation of children that followed. But with the coming of children and the prospect of living out one's life in the new land, provision for practice of the religious traditions of the old land assumed increasing importance. What started as a short trip to the new land to get rich quickly ended with permanent residence being established and the consequent need for religious service to be provided from the homeland.

While the above pattern holds true for many and perhaps most of the ethnic groups which settled in Canada, there were others who came to Canada to find religious freedom. Some of the early non-conformist Protestants and a number of the Muslims who reached Canada during the period 1950-1960 would be included in this group. But by far the most outstanding example, discussed in the conference, was that of the Mennonites. Two separate waves of what Frank Epp has called the "Dutch Mennonites" arrived in Canada from Russia. They came initially for religious reasons, but in the course of their trek to the new land they happened upon the best soil--which in the long run, produced business development and financial success, that then took centre stage in their lives. Such an outcome occurred not only to the two Dutch groups travelling from Russia, but also to many of the splinter groups that left established Mennonite communities in Pennsylvania, Southern Ontario and Manitoba and struck out for new land further West where a new religious start could be made. They too, frequently found good soil and, although

it was probably the last thing originally desired, they are now wealthy.
For many the trek to the new land for religious freedom and renewal has
ended instead in material prosperity. That material prosperity now
presents many challenges to the original religious ideal.

2. The Effect of Schools

As Frank Epp put it, "Institutions such as public or private
schools do much to strengthen or weaken the religious and ethnic qualities of minority groups." Evidence in support of this statement appeared from the experience of all the groups studied in the conference.
Very early in the history of Canada the various Roman Catholic groups
found it necessary to have their own school system. This same need has
been part of the Mennonite experience, and for many Mennonites the in-
ability to operate their own schools has caused them to move to a locality where this was possible. While this conference was being held
in Alberta during the summer of 1977 just such a problem was being
faced by a group of Alberta Mennonites who were being denied permission
to operate their own school.

The public school system, which until recently assumed the values
of the Protestant Anglo-Saxon majority culture, has proven itself to
be one of the most effective vehicles of Anglicization. Growing up as
a boy in the public school system of Southern Alberta, Leslie Kawamura
reports that he would sign himself as "Christian" on the school forms
in spite of his Japanese Buddhist heritage. For those who find it more
difficult to accommodate to the system, the public schools can pose
serious problems. In Southern Ontario, for example, there is the case
of Muslim girls being forced to wear shorts for Physical Education and
so expose their legs--which goes against the Muslim teaching. Cyril
Williams in discussing the Welsh experience has pointed out that Welsh
schools are essential for preservation of the Welsh culture and religion. All of this points to the need for provincial legislation and
financing which would allow the ethnic religious communities to operate
alternate schools. Only then would it really be true to say that the
religious ethnic communities in Canada have freedom to flourish.

Roger Hutchinson, in his stimulating and insightful paper, points
out that the large Anglo-Saxon Protestant denominations no longer find
their values to be co-extensive with those of the new technological
post-Christian society. Like the smaller ethnic religious groups discussed above, the large Protestant denominations such as the United,
Anglican and Presbyterian are beginning to reappear as minority groups

against the new background of a technological post-Christian society.
It is not surprising that some members within these new Protestant
minority groups are sensing the need for alternate schools of their
own. In Calgary, for example, there is currently a group of mainly
United Church background that has completed planning and is about to
launch an alternate Protestant Christian school system.

The conclusion with regard to the effect of schools on ethnic religious minority groups is unmistakable. There is a need for alternate schools if ethnic religious communities are to have the freedom
to flourish--to retain and further develop both their cultural ethnicity and their religious heritage. The transmission of the latter usually requires language training which allows for the continued recep-
tion of the sacred scriptures and devotional practices of a religious
tradition (e.g. Hebrew). The provision of such language training is a
major role which the alternate school can play in support of the religious tradition. For all of these reasons, both cultural and religious, the possibility of an alternate school system is an important
requirement for the survival of most religious ethnic communities.
There is some public recognition of this requirement in Alberta, at
least, in recent legislative and educational trends which allow for
"alternate schools".

3. The Leadership Problem

Difficulty in finding the right leadership is a problem which is
common to all religious ethnic communities, and it is a problem in both
the schools and the religious institutions. Virtually all of the early
ethnic religious groups settling in Canada suffered from the lack of
appropriate leadership. The first leadership was often supplied from
the home country. Although the formal training of such leadership was
often quite adequate, the needed empathy for the new land and the new
cultural situation was often lacking.

The solution to this problem seems to be in the training of second
and third generation children so that they become the new teachers and
religious leaders. As Leslie Kawamura's paper indicates, this is policy adopted by the Alberta Honpa Buddhist Church. Yvonne Haddad also
sees this as a move the Canadian Muslim communities must make.

4. Marriage

The conference discussion indicated that intermarriage is a common
problem for all groups in terms of both the ethnic and religious dimensions. Cyril Williams pointed out that it was due to intermarriage

that the Welsh language has been largely lost. In cases of intermarriage it is clear that the "melting pot effect" works, in the long run,
to the advantage of the majority or host religion and culture. Those
groups that assimilate well (e.g. the Japanese Buddhists) see this as
less of a problem than others. As Leslie Kawamura indicates in his
paper, Buddhism has no racial or cultural attachment and is therefore
able to adapt to intermarriage successfully. Others, such as the Muslims, view this situation with considerable alarm. For the Muslims the
problem is one where their own marriage law is at variance with that of
the secular society in which they now live. The status of women, the
procedure for divorce and many other issues become matters for debate.

Grant Maxwell's study points out that in Roman Catholic groups
there is a change underway with regard to marriage values. Some ninety
percent say "yes" to a lifetime marriage, two-thirds say "yes" to premarital sex, and fifty-five percent only say "yes" to childbearing.
Maxwell concludes that these answers seem to represent a blending of
traditional Catholic standards with modern secular mores.

5. Tension Between the Generations

It is perhaps inevitable that there will be tension between the
first generation settlers of a religious ethnic group and the succeed-
ing generations. While the first generation still lives, as it were,
with "one foot" in the old country, their children and grandchildren
live almost completely in the new land. It is to be expected, therefore, that tensions would result. In the Japanese Buddhist community
there is frequently a loss of the Japanese language in the second and
third generations. In the Muslim community the tension is focussed
when old country Imams travel through the country and condemn many of
the practices that the Canadian communities develop. In such situations the Imams are usually the functional equivalent of the first generation viewpoint.

In his analysis of Canadian Roman Catholic ethnic groups Grant
Maxwell found that age was the most significant distinguishing factor
in the opinions expressed. This he found to be especially true of religious beliefs and ethical standards.

6. Attraction to the Notion of "Multiculturalism"

Most of the conference speakers exhibited an attraction to the notion of "multiculturalism" as presenting a possible solution or practical model under which religious ethnic communities could live successfully. Yet at the same time there was a realization that any

multiculturalism attempt runs the risk of being openly or subtly over-
powered by the dominant host culture or ideology. Roger Hutchinson, in
his paper *Religion, Ethnicity and Public Policy*, shows how just such a
subtle overpowering by the dominant Anglo-Saxon Protestant culture
worked against established German-Catholic prairie communities that
were bypassed by the railway. Hutchinson points out that in 1936 Dawson was counselling just such a "subtle approach" as an effective method for assimilating religious ethnic minority groups into the dominant
Anglo-Saxon culture. Hutchinson also suggests that the current Federal
Government's emphasis on multiculturalism, although seeming sincere on
the surface, may in effect be functioning as a smoke-screen to hide the
old Anglo-conformity model of immigrant assimilation that Dawson had
earlier championed. Current Federal Multiculturalism policies deal
with instruction in a second language, modes of dress and weekend recreation behaviour. Folk-dances, food-fairs, ethnic restaurants and
traditional costumes are encouraged and given financial subsidization.
But, as Hutchinson makes clear, such multilculturalism activities do
not challenge our dominant cultural and economic attitudes. Nor do
they change the accepted Anglo-Saxon standard of what is required to
be a success in Canada. Worst yet they may be merely shallow, romantic
diversions which treat traditions other than Anglo-Saxon, as enriching
Canada mainly through their entertainment value. Perhaps this is why
there is increasing resistance among the Canadian Indian tribes against
showing their sacred dances and songs in a white cultural setting,
where they will be robbed of their depth and treated as shallow entertainment. In Hutchinson's view evidence of a sincere commitment to
multiculturalism would be a shift in the reigning consensus which undergirds Canada's current economy and technological society. It is in prophetic protest against the injustice imposed by the reigning secular
system that Hutchinson sees the mainline Protestant denominations join-
ing forces with the religious ethnic minorities. It is Hutchinson's
hope that this new coming together of the large Protestant churches and
the smaller ethnic groups will be for more than just protest purposes.
It could provide Canadian religion and Canadian society with a basis
for multiculturalism that would be truly effective.

II. Points of Difference

Although there was a surprisingly large segment of common experience among the diverse groups studied by the conference, some definite
differences also appeared.

1. Strategies for Survival

Among the ethnic religious groups studied a variety of strategies
for survival were apparent. At the one extreme were those who actively
aimed at assimilation; at the other extreme were those who actively opposed assimilation in any form.

A good example of the active assimilators would be the Southern
Alberta Japanese Pure Land Buddhist group described in Leslie Kawamura's
paper. Their strategy would seem to have been successful. Although on
the surface their religious activity seems to closely approximate typical Anglo-Saxon Protestant forms--complete with ministers, congregations, Sunday services, Sunday schools, women's groups and church pic-
nics--a careful analysis of the content embodied in the form shows it
to be authentic Buddhism. Yet in the eyes of the Anglo-Saxon Protestant communities in which they live, these Japanese Pure Land Buddhists
are judged to have "fitted-in" and taken their place as responsible
members of the community. Another assimilation example would be provided by the Hungarian Catholics who expect the first generation to
remain true to the old country language and traditions, but who are
apparently quite happy for the children to be assimilated and to affil-
iate with a regular English Catholic congregation.

The opposite strategy of non-assimilation can be broken down into
at least two sub-categories. There are those who resist assimilation
by isolating themselves into a self-sufficient colony. As Frank Epp
described it, the colony approach has shown itself to be the most successful in preserving Mennonite values and ethnicity in Canada. Because colonies with large tracts of land and virtually complete control
over education, service functions such as electricity, roads, etc. are
becoming increasingly impossible in Canada, many of the Colony Mennonites are currently seeking to leave Canada and relocate in Latin America. Another contemporary example of the colony strategy against assimilation is seen in the stance being adopted by many Canadian Indian
tribes in their desire to take over complete control on their reserves.

A quite different strategy of non-assimilation is adopted by those
who seek to protect themselves by transforming or converting the dominant host culture to their viewpoint. Perhaps the best example here is
provided by Yvonne Haddad's description of the approach being adopted
by the leadership of the Canadian Islamic community--especially under
the influence of the conservative Indo-Pakistani element. Haddad points
out that the leadership of the Islamic community has become aware that
it cannot passively accept the *status quo* of accelerated assimilation

of the young into the secular culture of Canada. Consequently, the educational emphasis in the mosques will shift from passive receptivity
to a tactic of active rejection of that which is against the Muslim
tradition. As Haddad puts it, "What is being sought is not the maintenance of an ethnic identity but the projection of a new world order
where all humanity is invited to participate in Islam in commitment to
God, a commitment which would eradicate all ethnic, national or cultural differences." This approach is clearly completely opposed to
any notion of the dignity and respect which the approach of multiculturalism requires be given to each ethnic religious group. The goal
in the developing Muslim approach is to resist assimilation into the
host culture by absorbing and reforming it (along with all other ethnic religious groups currently existing), so that it may conform to
the religious ideals of Islam.

Although one may question the practicality and the potentiality
for success of this desire "to assimilate the assimilators", one must
agree with Haddad when she concludes that this approach should not be
viewed as a regression into ethnocentrism. Rather, it should be viewed as an attempt to transcend the "tribalism" of race and as an invitation into theo-centrism. "This avenue" she concludes, "appears to
be the only option available given the uncompromising commitment to
ideal Islam and the anti-Arab, anti-Pakistani, anti-Muslim attitude of
Canadian society."

Frank Epp points out that both the assimilation and isolationist
strategies, along with many combinations of the two approaches are to
be found among the Mennonites. But when the Mennonite takes seriously
its mission to preach the gospel to all the world, both of these approaches pose problems. The assimilators successfully learn the language and culture of the host group and so can communicate and gain
converts. But once the converts are gained there is no unique community to keep them, due to the thoroughness of the assimilation. The isolationist groups have the opposite problem. They succeed in preserving
the community of faith, but their very isolation makes successful
preaching and conversion virtually impossible. The dilemma of the isolationist group is that by isolating themselves so as to preserve the
community they effectively cut themselves off from their mission. This
would seem to be a common problem for all minority religious ethnic
groups possessing a divine directive to mission. It will be a serious
problem for all Christian and Muslim groups. It may be less of a problem for Jews, Hindus and Buddhists.

2. Language

The subtle way in which the dominant language of a host culture
can work against religious minorities may be seen in the very anglicization of their names, e.g. Hindu, Welsh, Indian. In each of these
examples the group named disowns the anglicization as incorrect and
derogatory. In this context there are two questions to be raised:
(1) Is the retention of a sacred language necessary for religious
survival and vitality?; (2) Is the retention of an ethnic language
necessary for cultural survival of the minority group? The answers to
both of these questions by most of the religious ethnic groups being
considered would seem to be "yes". The notable exception would seem to
be the very pro-assimilation Japanese Buddhists--and this may well be
because Buddhism is the only religion (of those being discussed) that
does not base itself upon a scriptural revelation.

For many of the groups examined the old adage, "He who loses his
language loses his faith." seems to apply. The sacred language is seen
by many as the saving factor that resists assimilation and safeguards
the heart of the religion (i.e. its revelation and devotional hymns).
This viewpoint would certainly hold true for Hindus, Muslims, Jews, and
North American Indians. In many cases it is an approach that is seen
to be equally true for the transmission of ones culture. Referring to
the experience of the Welsh, Cyril Williams says that language is more
than just a means of communication--it is a nations memory and its consciousness.

Another possibility with regard to language is that ethnic religious minorities require a special kind of bilingualism--one language
for the religious purposes of scripture and devotion, and another language (the language of the host culture) for secular assimilation purposes. This approach seems to be popular with many of Canada's Mennonites, Muslims, Hindus and Jews. In the case of the Dutch Mennonites,
for example, high German is used for worship and kept pure while low
German and English come to function for everyday secular purposes. For
most Muslims Arabic is the language of scripture and prayer while English is used otherwise. The same sort of practice applies to Hindus,
with Sanskrit being held sacred, and to the reverence of classical Hebrew by the Jews. This approach is of course not unknown to English
protestants who in the recent past viewed the King James Version of the
Bible as a kind of sacred language, not to be corrupted by the changing
expressions of everyday secular English. While this bilingual compromise seems to offer the advantage of safeguarding the religious

tradition, it does tend to result in the splitting of one's world into
two parts, the sacred and the secular. Whether or not this is seen as
a serious problem probably depends on one's theological position. If
one operates from a strongly transcendentalist theological position
then the split between the sacred and the secular may be widened until
the bilingual solution to the minority ethnic problem is rendered dis-
functional.

     In contrast to all of the above is the Buddhist approach which
seems to avoid many of the problems which arise when language is viewed
as divine, or, at least, as uniquely revealing the divine. For the
Buddhist, language is merely one of many conventional forms of communication which may or may not be helpful in pointing to the reality which
is being witnessed to and experienced. Since that reality is universally present, it can just as easily be pointed to with English words
as with Japanese, Chinese, Sanskrit or Pali. Indeed, in the end, the
"thusness" or "thatness" that is pointed to requires that one transcend
the conceptual limitations of language itself and achieve a direct experience of the universally present reality. Often gestures and acts
may prove more helpful than words. Consequently, it is not surprising,
and it is quite consistent, that the True Pure Land Japanese Buddhist
Church of Alberta should decide that once the first generation Japanese
have died, the English language of the dominant culture will be both
fully adequate and most appropriate for all purposes. Here there is
certainly no sense of separation between the sacred and the secular,
nor is there any problem perceived in a fully assimilationist approach.

3. Problems with Definitions

     It is evident that one of the obstacles to ongoing scholarship on
the question of religion and ethnicity is the difficulty in agreeing
on the meaning of the two key terms. In some of the papers (e.g. the
papers by Goa, Hutchinson and Epp) the term religion seems to be defined
in such a way as to also include any ideology. "Religion" seems "reduced" or "expanded" from its classical meaning of a "religious tradition" to any "ultimate concern". The difficulty here is that the term
"religion" becomes so general and inclusive as to frustrate further academic analysis.

     The term "ethnicity" when taken in relation to religion also proves
difficult to define. On the one hand there is the helpful suggestion
from the Jewish tradition that ethnicity should be thought of as a
"Peoplehood"--a religious people with a sense of mission or calling, a

calling which would protect against assimilation. The Islamic tradition puts forth a quite different suggestion, namely, that Islam is
understood as One People (viewed as including all mankind) under God.
"Ethnicity", in this approach, is effectively first put under the umbrella of religion and is finally completely absorbed by religion.

The definitional problems involved in the academic use of both
"religion" and "ethnicity" remain unresolved.

4. The Current Situation

Several different views are to be found with regard to the current
situation of religious ethnic minorities in Canada. Roger Hutchinson
hopes for the development of a true and honest multiculturalism but
fears that the religious minorities (including the mainline protestant
denominations) will be absorbed into the new ideology of post-Christian
secular industrial society. Grant Maxwell sees the future of the ethnic and religious minorities as being caught up in the renewal movements which he finds in the under thirty age group. Harold Barclay
points out that multiculturalism and Islam simply will not go together.
Beyond the Muslim ideal of transforming all of Canada into "One People
under Allah" there seems no obvious solution to the problem.

Frank Epp suggests that although it seems as if the ethnic minorities are vanishing and being wiped out by the Twentieth Century, it is
equally evident that a plethora of new minorities are emerging. Although the hope immediately after World War II was for the establishment of a World Community headed by the United Nations, the reality is
that a host of new natinalisms and minorities have arisen. They are
ideological or religious minorities that are seeking rights, demanding
their place in the sun, and determined not to be swallowed up by any
other group. The existence of a large number of such groups is now the
challenge to Canada, and, on a larger scale, to the world. In the face
of this increasing pluralism Epp sees the major challenge ahead as the
helping of these new minority groups to feel that they are part of Canada. Otherwise, the outcome, in some instances at least, may well be
guerilla warfare. In this situation the religions, and more specifically the older ethnic religious groups with their past experience in
just such situations, have an important role to play--to help all groups
large or small to come together as brothers.

56493

56493

BL
2530
.C2W67   RELIGION AND ETHNICITY /

AUTHOR
1977   ed. Harold Coward and
TITLE   Leslie Kawamura

DEMCO